...oved.
...e moved once every
...o years since I came
...o Tokyo. My parents
and editor think I just like
moving, but I don't. I just
get tired of things quickly
and after two years I feel
like going somewhere else.

-Tite Kubo

BLEACH is author Tite Kubo's second title. Kubo made his debut with ZOMBIEPOWDER., a four-volume series for WEEKLY SHONEN JUMP. To date, BLEACH has been translated into numerous languages and has also inspired an animated TV series that began airing in the U.S. in 2006. Beginning its serialization in 2001, BLEACH is still a mainstay in the pages of WEEKLY SHONEN JUMP. In 2005, BLEACH was awarded the prestigious Shogakukan Manga Award in the *shonen* (boys) category.

BLEACH
Vol. 26: The Mascaron Drive
The SHONEN JUMP Manga Edition

This volume contains material that was originally published in SHONEN JUMP #72-74. Artwork in the magazine may have been altered slightly from what is presented in this volume.

STORY AND ART BY
TITE KUBO

English Adaptation/Lance Caselman
Translation/Joe Yamazaki
Touch-Up Art & Lettering/Mark McMurray
Design/Sean Lee
Editor/Pancha Diaz

Editor in Chief, Books/Alvin Lu
Editor in Chief, Magazines/Marc Weidenbaum
VP, Publishing Licensing/Rika Inouye
VP, Sales & Product Marketing/Gonzalo Ferreyra
VP, Creative/Linda Espinosa
Publisher/Hyoe Narita

BLEACH © 2001 by Tite Kubo. All rights reserved. First published in Japan in 2001 by SHUEISHA Inc., Tokyo. English translation rights arranged by SHUEISHA Inc. The stories, characters and incidents mentioned in this publication are entirely fictional.

No portion of this book may be reproduced or transmitted in any form or by any means without written permission from the copyright holders.

The rights of the author(s) of the work(s) in this publication to be so identified have been asserted in accordance with the Copyright, Designs and Patents Act 1988. A CIP catalogue record for this book is available from the British Library.

Printed in the U.S.A.

Published by VIZ Media, LLC
P.O. Box 77010
San Francisco, CA 94107

SHONEN JUMP Manga Edition
10 9 8 7 6 5 4 3 2 1
First printing, March 2009

PARENTAL ADVISORY
BLEACH is rated T for Teen and is recommended for ages 13 and up. This volume contains fantasy violence.

ratings.viz.com

THE WORLD'S MOST POPULAR MANGA

Next Volume Preview

ORIHIME IS MY FRIEND.
I'LL SAVE HER ALL BY MYSELF.

Orihime is kidnapped by the Arrancar Ulquiorra! The Soul Reapers see her as a traitor and refuse to let Ichigo rescue her. Ichigo will never abandon his friend, but now he's up against the entire Hueco Mundo!

Read it first in SHONEN JUMP magazine!

WHAT'S THIS?
WHO ARE THESE FOOLS?

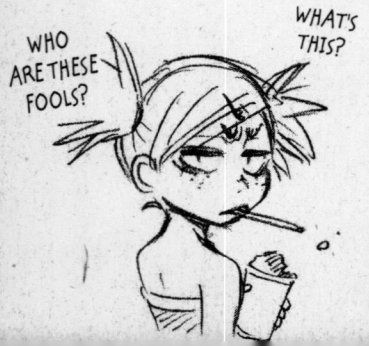

CONTINUED IN BLEACH 27

WHOOM
RIP
THESE SOUL REAPERS ARE MORE...
...IN-COMPETENT THAN I THOUGHT.
KREEK
THEY DON'T SEEM TO REALIZE...
...THAT THE PASSAGE IS THE MOST DANGEROUS PART.

WE'LL ESCORT YOU.
NO, THAT'S OKAY...
HUH ?!
YOU'RE NOT A RYOKA ANYMORE. YOU'RE OUR GUEST!
IT'S CUSTOMARY FOR TWO SOUL REAPERS WITH THEIR HELL BUTTERFLIES REMOVED TO ACCOMPANY A GUEST THROUGH THE PASSAGE!
I KNOW IT'S A NUISANCE, BUT PLEASE INDULGE US!
OKAY ...
THEN ... THANKS.
I'D BETTER HURRY...
IT'S OKAY. I GOT A LITTLE STRONG-ER OVER THE LAST MONTH.
I KNOW I CAN HELP OUT NOW!
SO HOLD ON, ICHIGO...
AND EVERYONE ELSE!
HMPH.
ONLY TWO GUARDS.

DOOM
MS. INOUE!
MS. ORIHIME INOUE!
THE OUTER WALL OF THE DANGAI HAS BEEN STABILIZED!
YOU CAN PASS THROUGH NOW!!
THANK YOU!
DASH
THANK YOU SO MUCH!!
TMP
!

SKRRSHHHHH
AH!
WHOA.
THAT ONE'S KIND OF WEIRD.
AH...
!

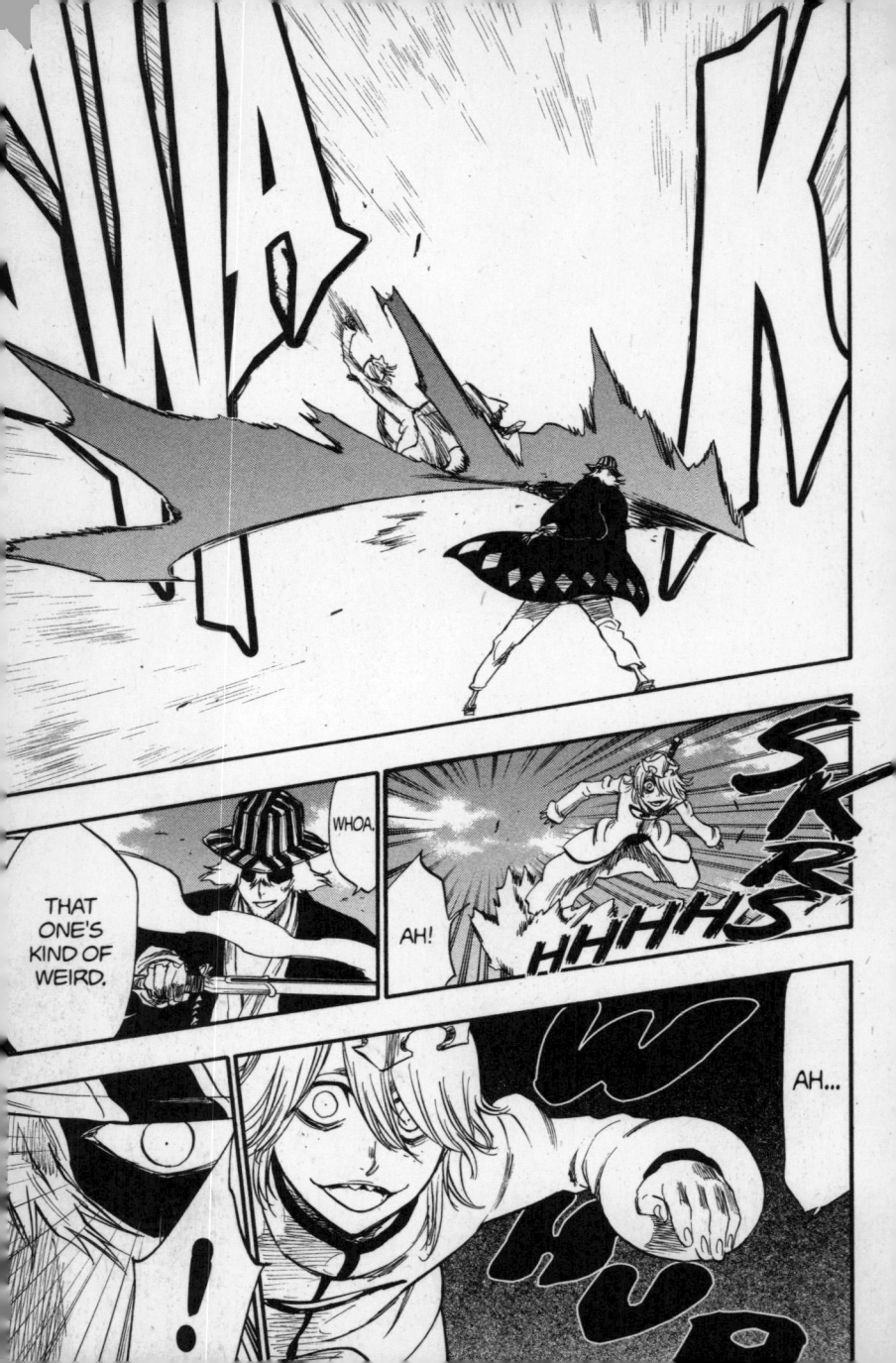

OH!
FORGIVE ME. I SHOULD INTRODUCE MYSELF.
I'M KISUKE URAHARA.
I RUN A DINKY LITTLE CANDY STORE CALLED URAHARA SHÔTEN.
I'M DE-LIGHTED ...
...TO MAKE YOUR ACQUAIN-TANCE.

PHEW
...
JUST IN TIME.
THAT WAS CLOSE.
KLUNK
...
WHO ARE YOU?

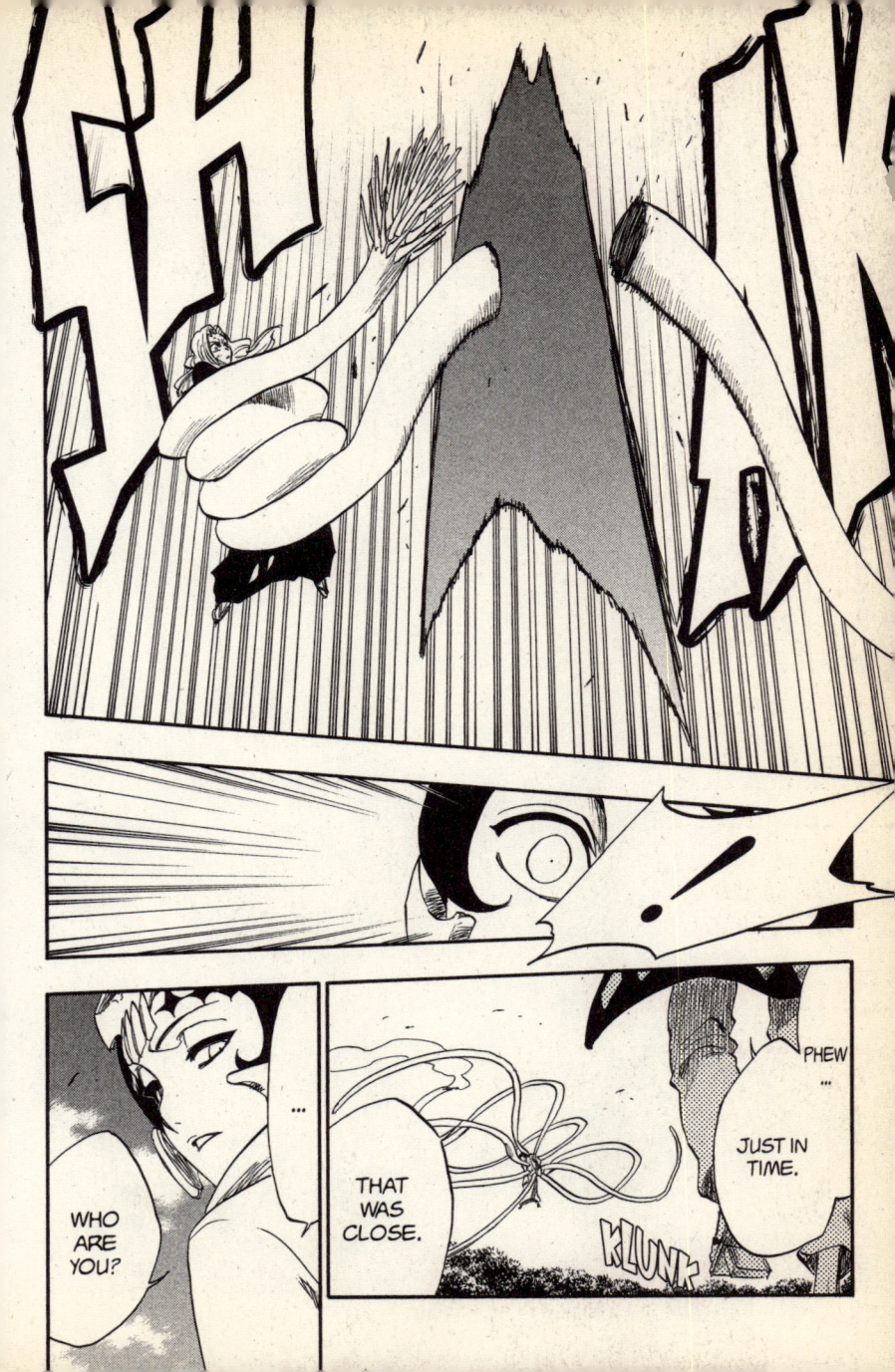

MAYBE I'LL...
!
...POKE IT FULL OF HOLES.

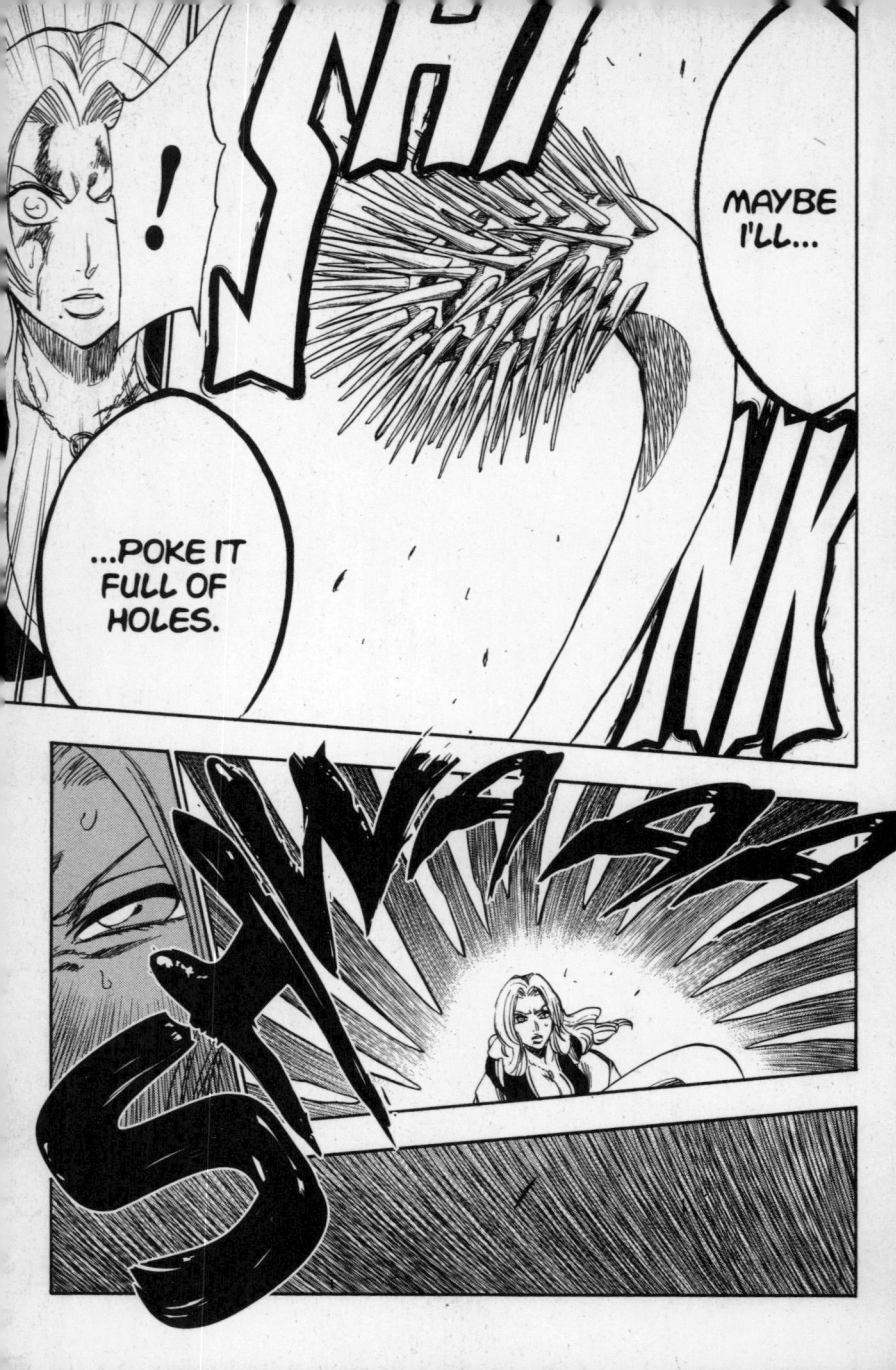

UGH!!
YUMICHIKA!! MATSU-MOTO!!
AGH!!
SHWAP
YOU KNOW WHAT, LADY?
YOU'VE GOT A KILLER BODY.
KREK
WOW...
IT'S LUSCIOUS.
WHUP

WMMM
WHAP
OH...
WMM WMM
...
HUH?
AHH
URGH!!
I'VE GOT NOTHING TO DO!

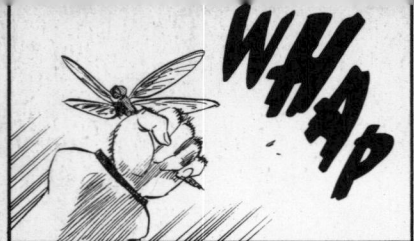

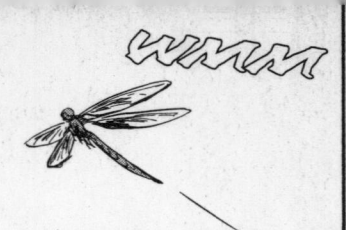

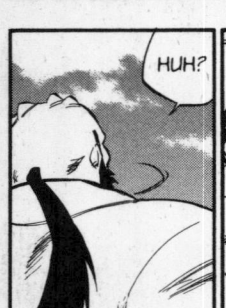

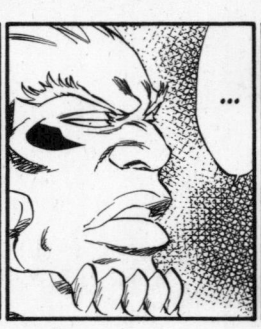

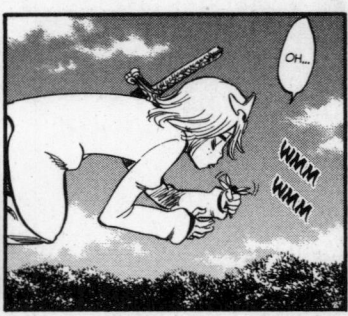

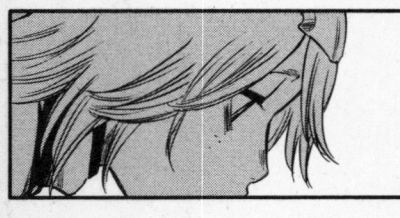

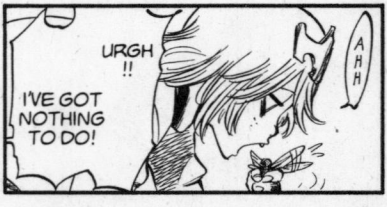

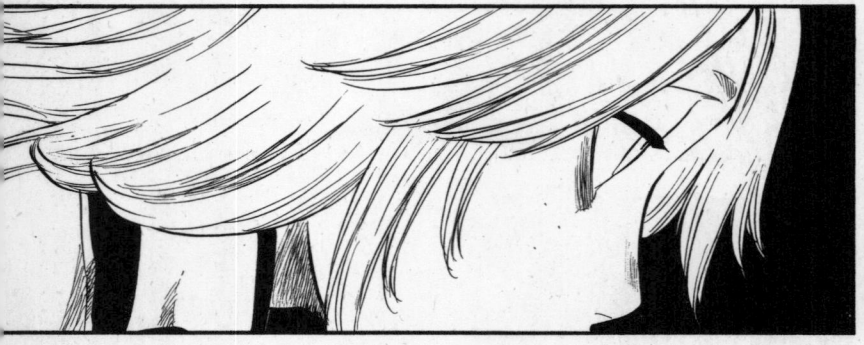

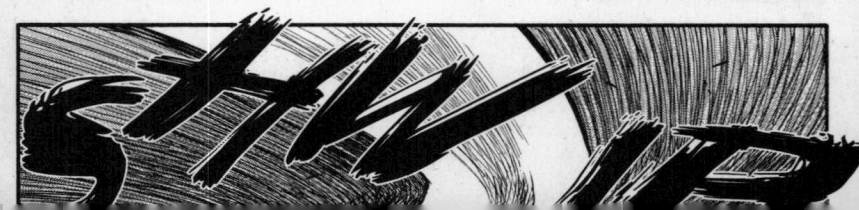

WOOSH
UGH...
THERE'S NOTHING TO DO...
THAT LUPPI STOLE THOSE SOUL REAPERS FROM ME.
BUT IT'S A PAIN TO GO LOOK FOR OTHER ONES.
YAAAAWN...
HEY!
ROOKIE!
WHAT'RE YOU DOING?!
WMM

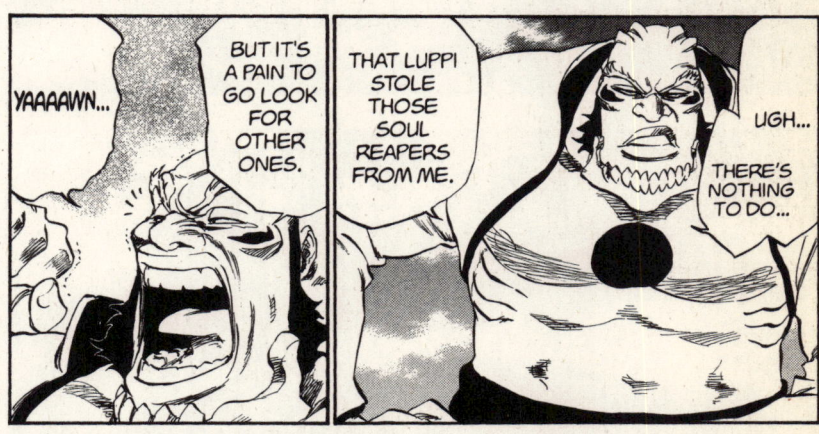

DO OM
WHUP
WHUP
WHUP
GEEZ...
THIS IS PATHETIC.
ARE YOU GUYS REALLY OFFICERS OF THE THIRTEEN COURT GUARD COMPANIES?
THW IP
BOOO-
-RING.

HUFF...
HUFF...
HUFF...

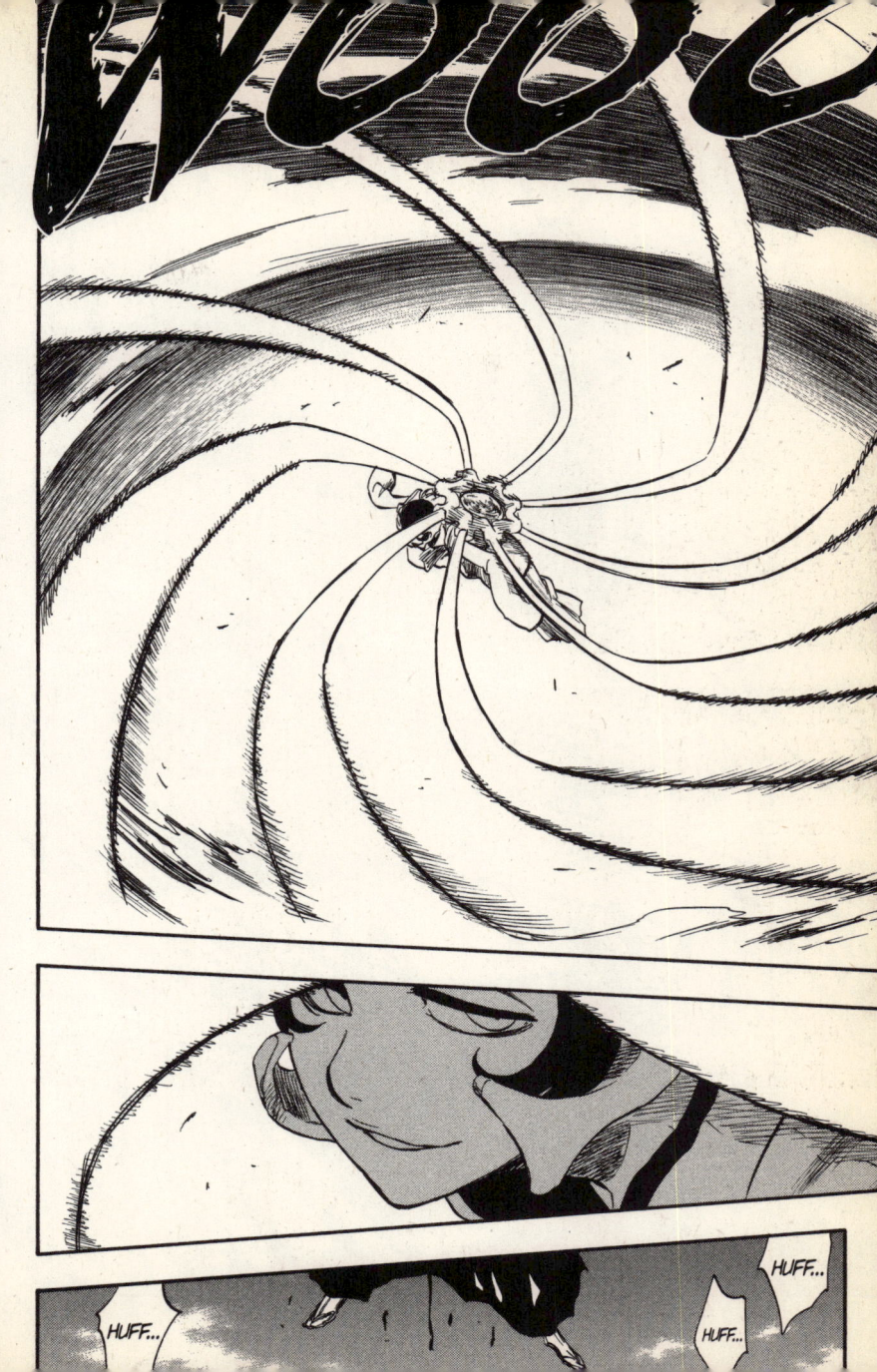

SHWAK
WHAM
WHAM
WHAM
WHAM
WHAM
WHAM

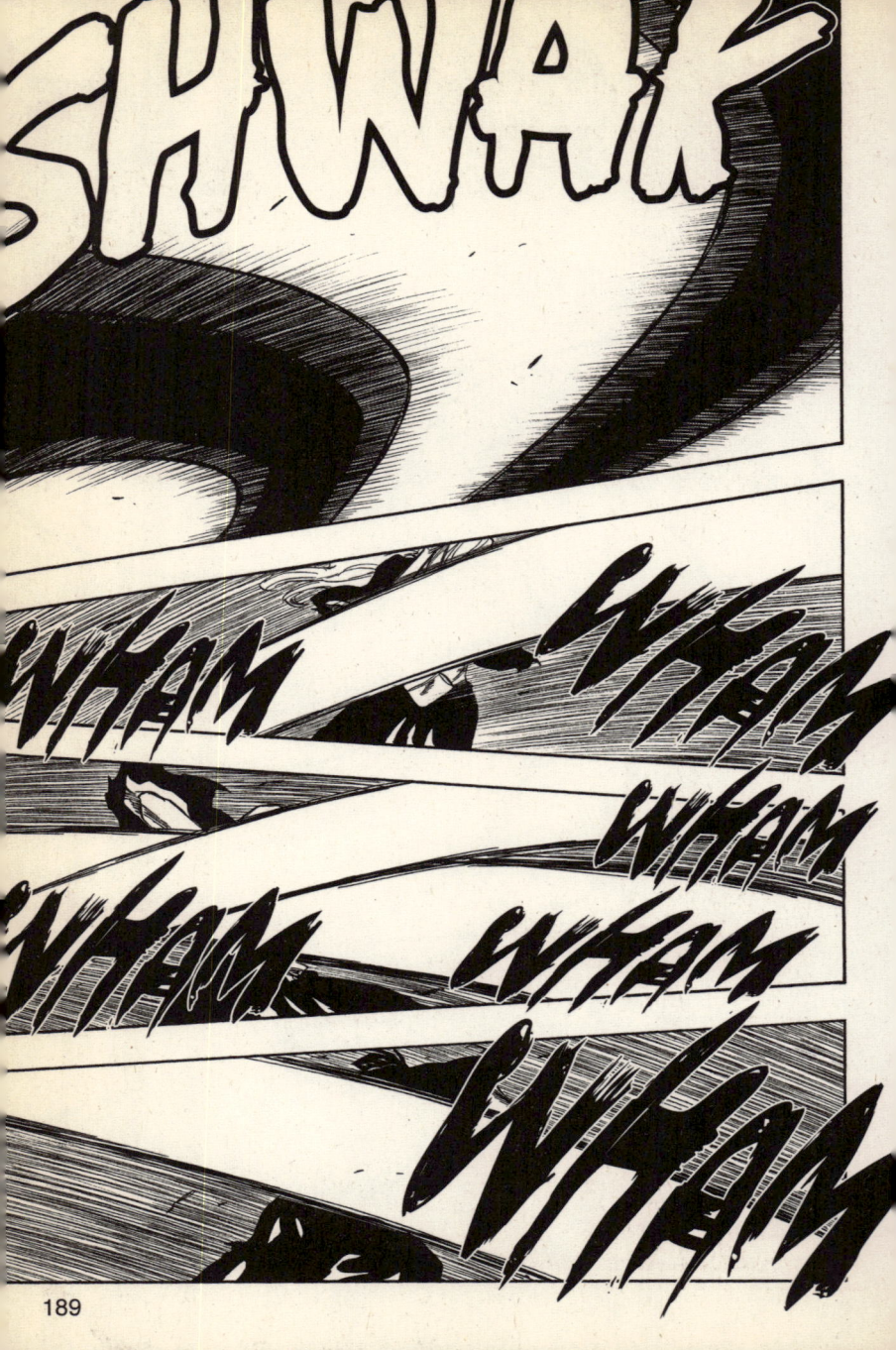

BLEACH. 233. El Violador

KPANG
LOOKS LIKE...
...YOU USED UP ALL YOUR POWER.
YOU GOT SHORT OF BREATH THE INSTANT YOUR MASK CAME OFF!
IT'S OVER, SOUL REAPER!
I'M HURT PRETTY BAD MYSELF, BUT...
...IN THE END, EVEN WITH THAT POWER OF YOURS...
YOU COULDN'T...
...BEAT ME!!

DOON

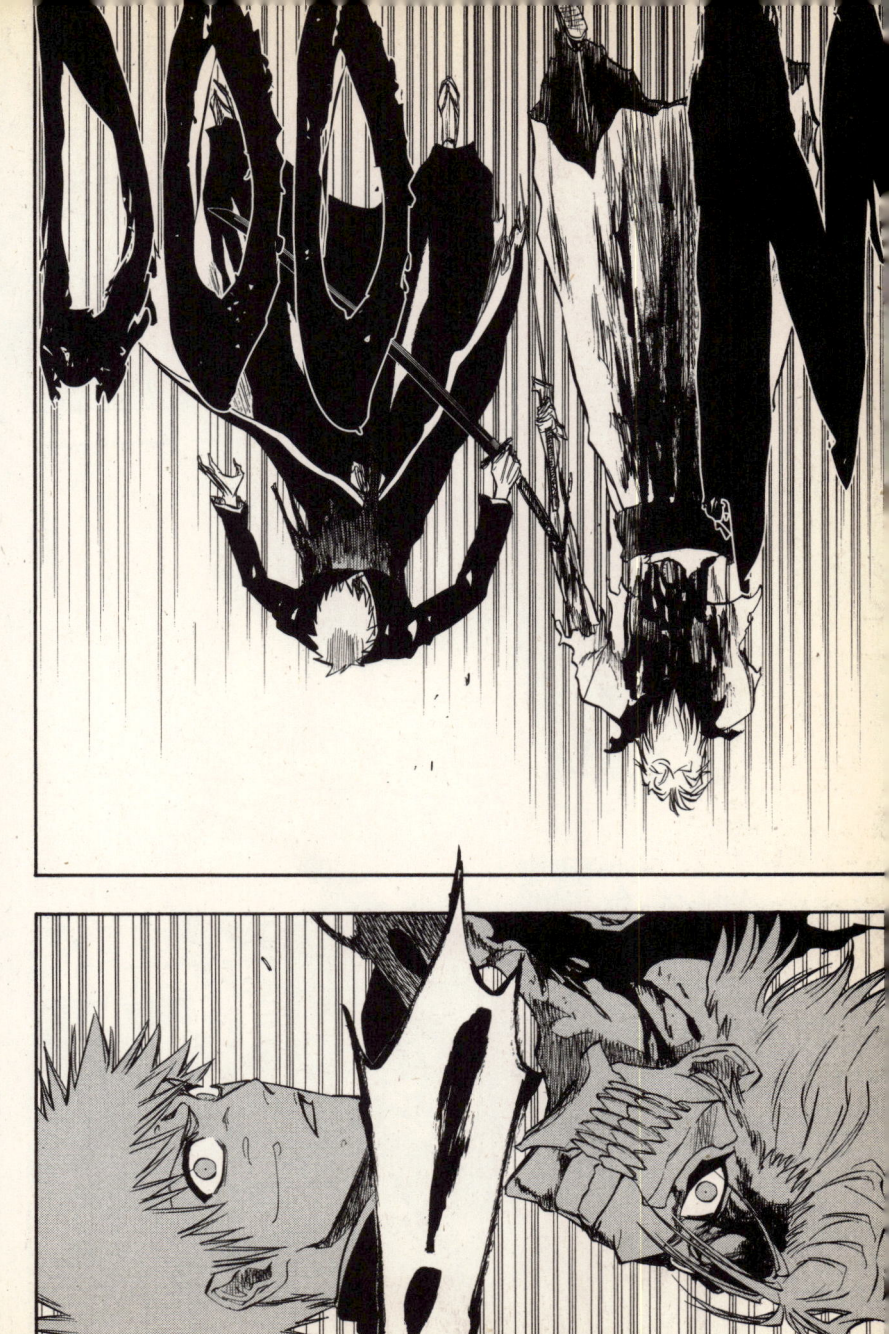

233. El Violador

NO...
MY MASK!

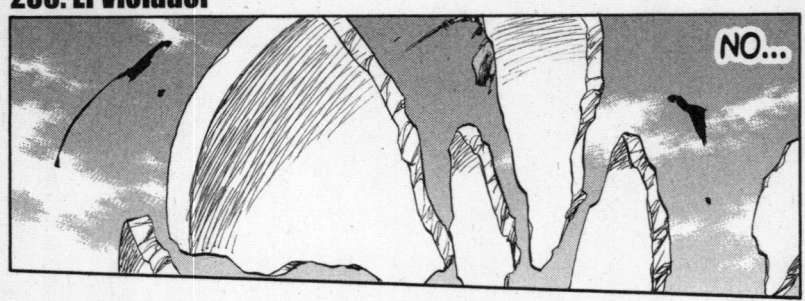

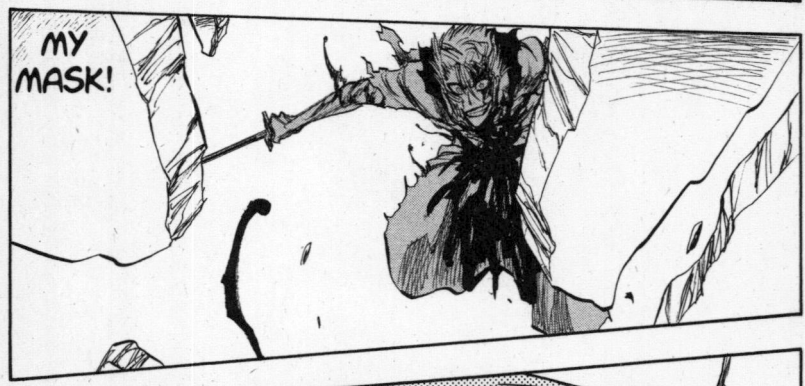

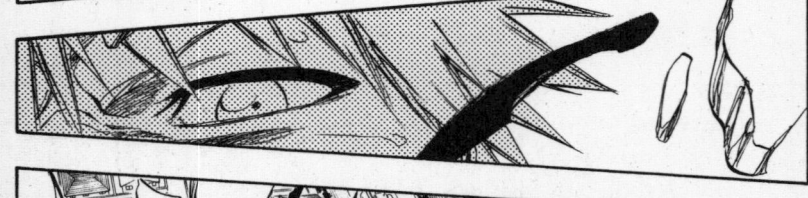

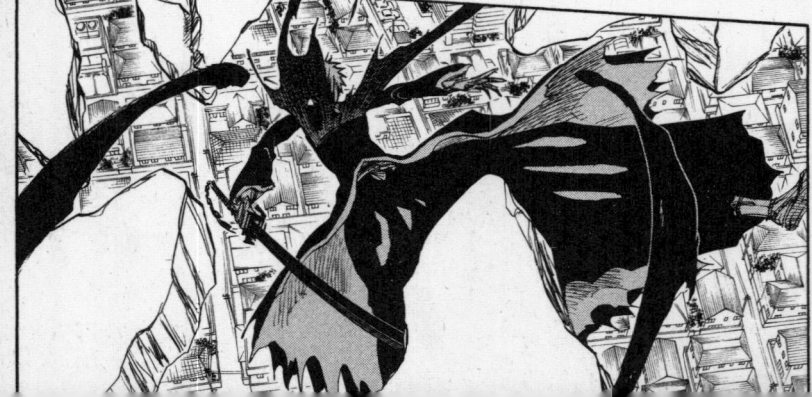

I'VE DECIDED ON THIS ONE.
WHAT'S THE DIFFERENCE? WHY DON'T YOU GO WITH THAT ONE, ISANE?
WHAT'S THE DIFFERENCE?!
BU... BUT, CAPTAIN ...!
GO WITH THAT ONE...
... ISANE.
Y...
YES, MA'AM ...
I'M SORRY.

IT'S OVER...
SOUL REAPER !!
SHWAK

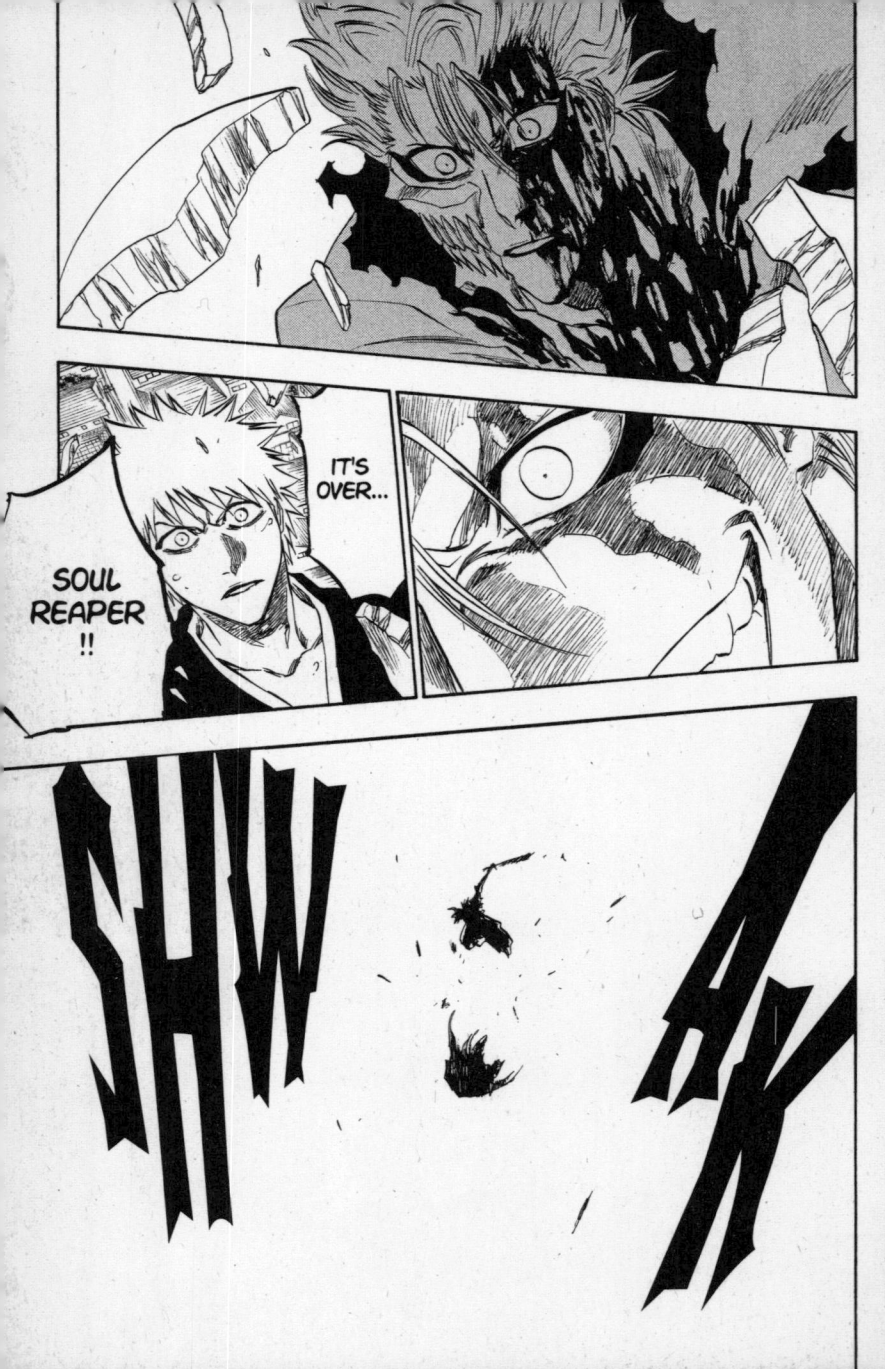

MY MASK !!!

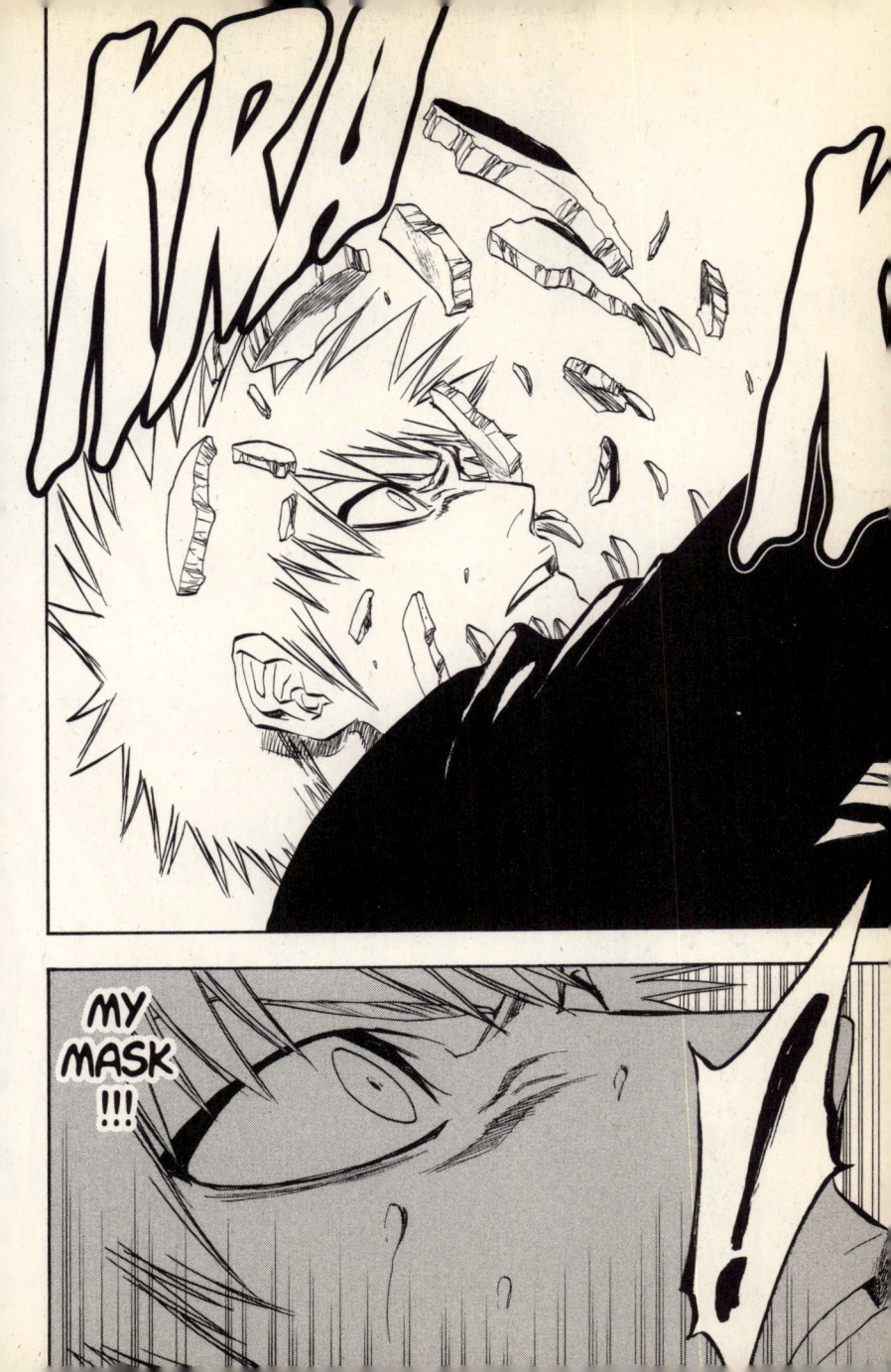

BOOM
KLANK
HMPH!
IT'S OVER ...
...GRIMM-JOW.

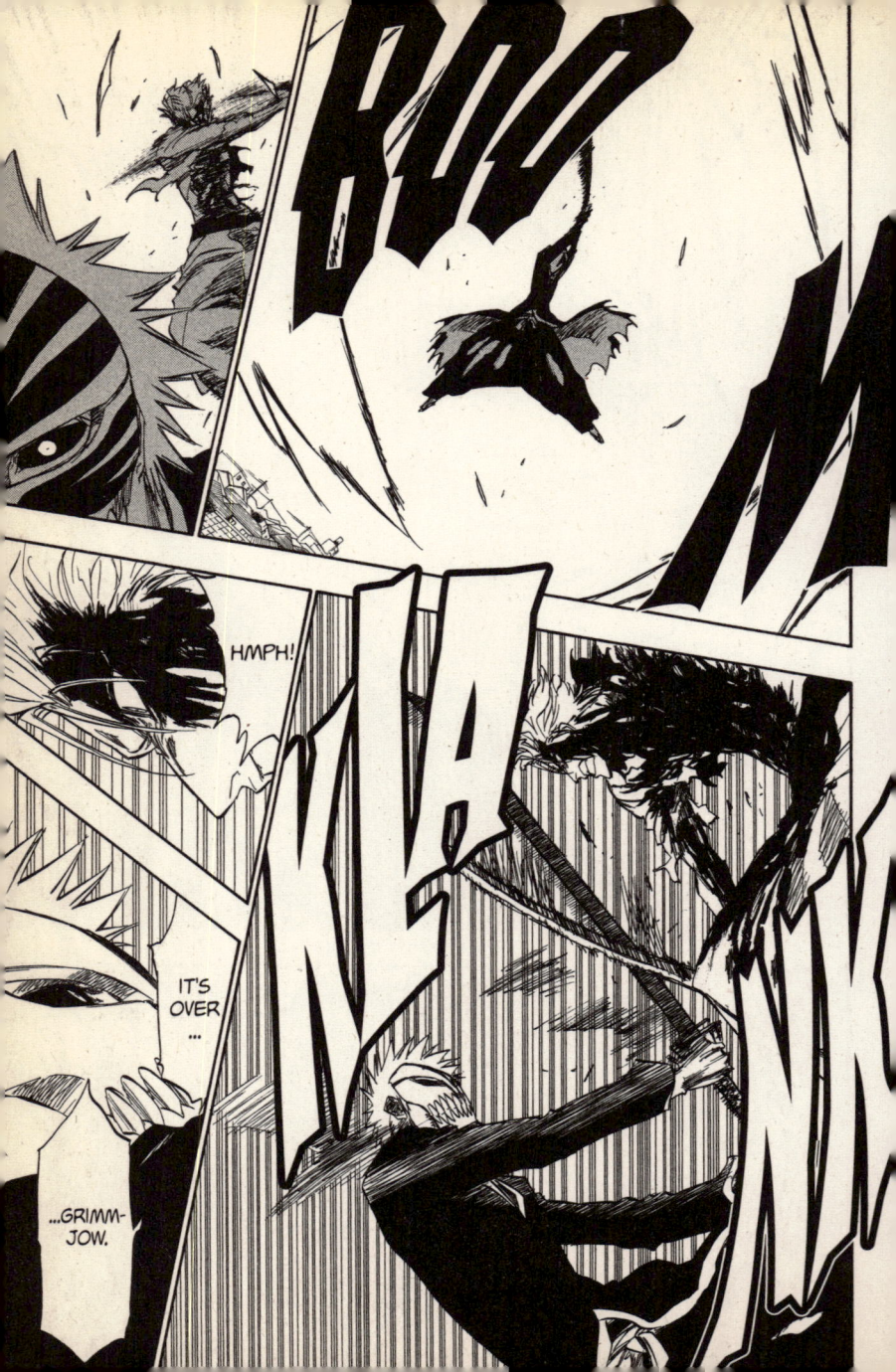

THWANG
AH...
DRMMMMMM
GRAAAH

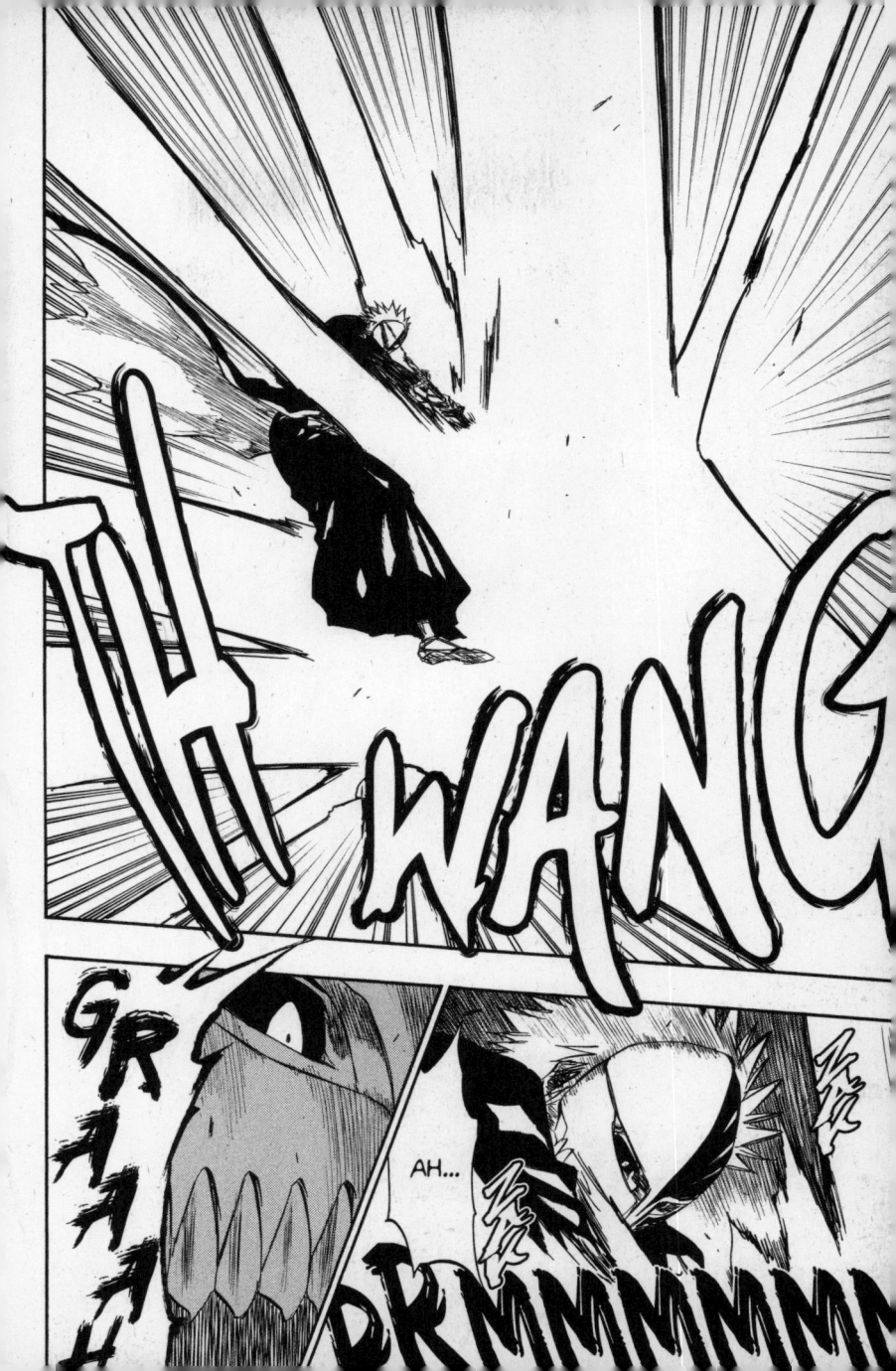

WHOOF
Y...
YOU...
...LITTLE JERK !!
DOOM BLAST !!

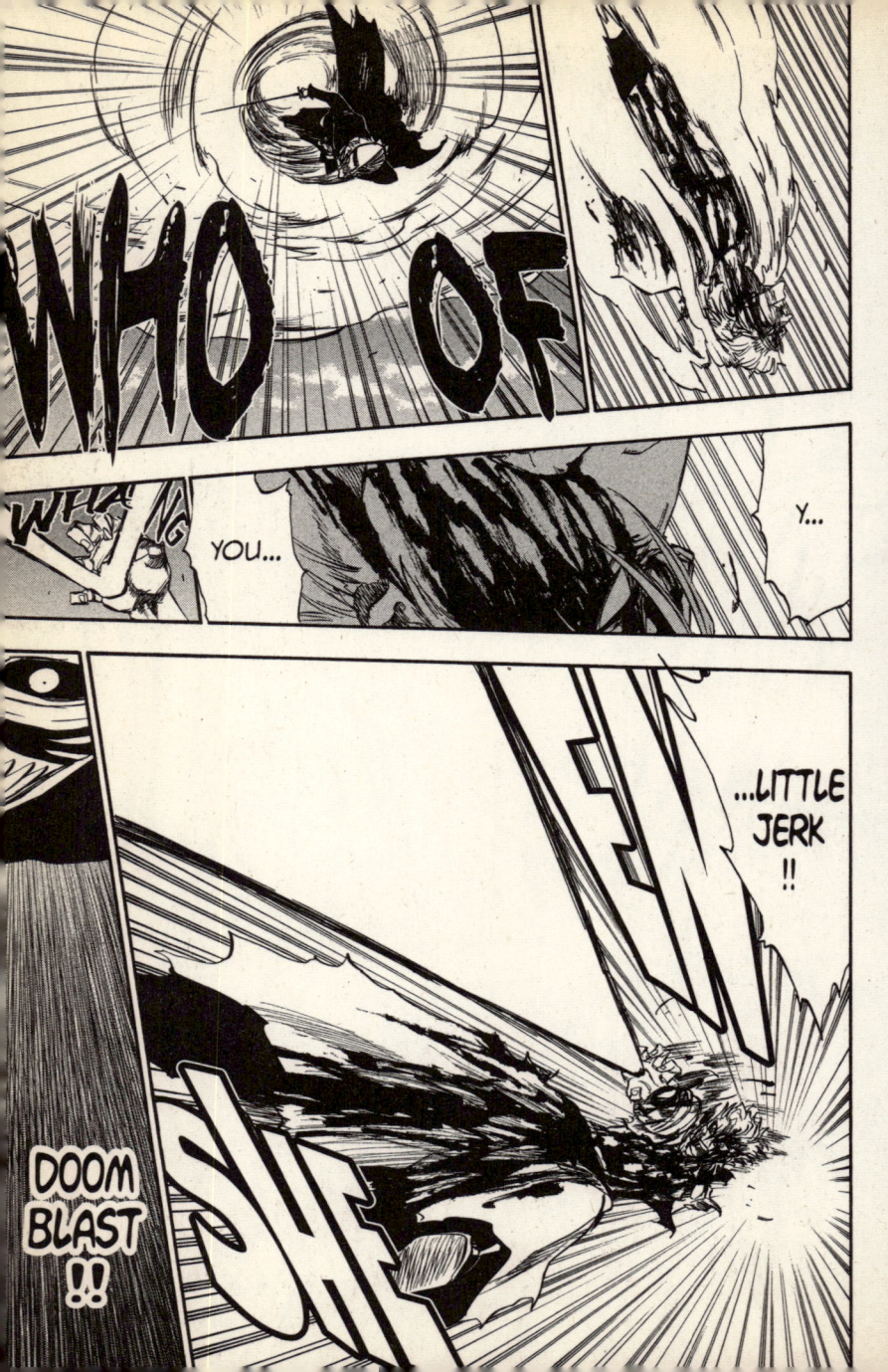

I DON'T HAVE TIME TO EXPLAIN.
SHWAK
FWOOSH

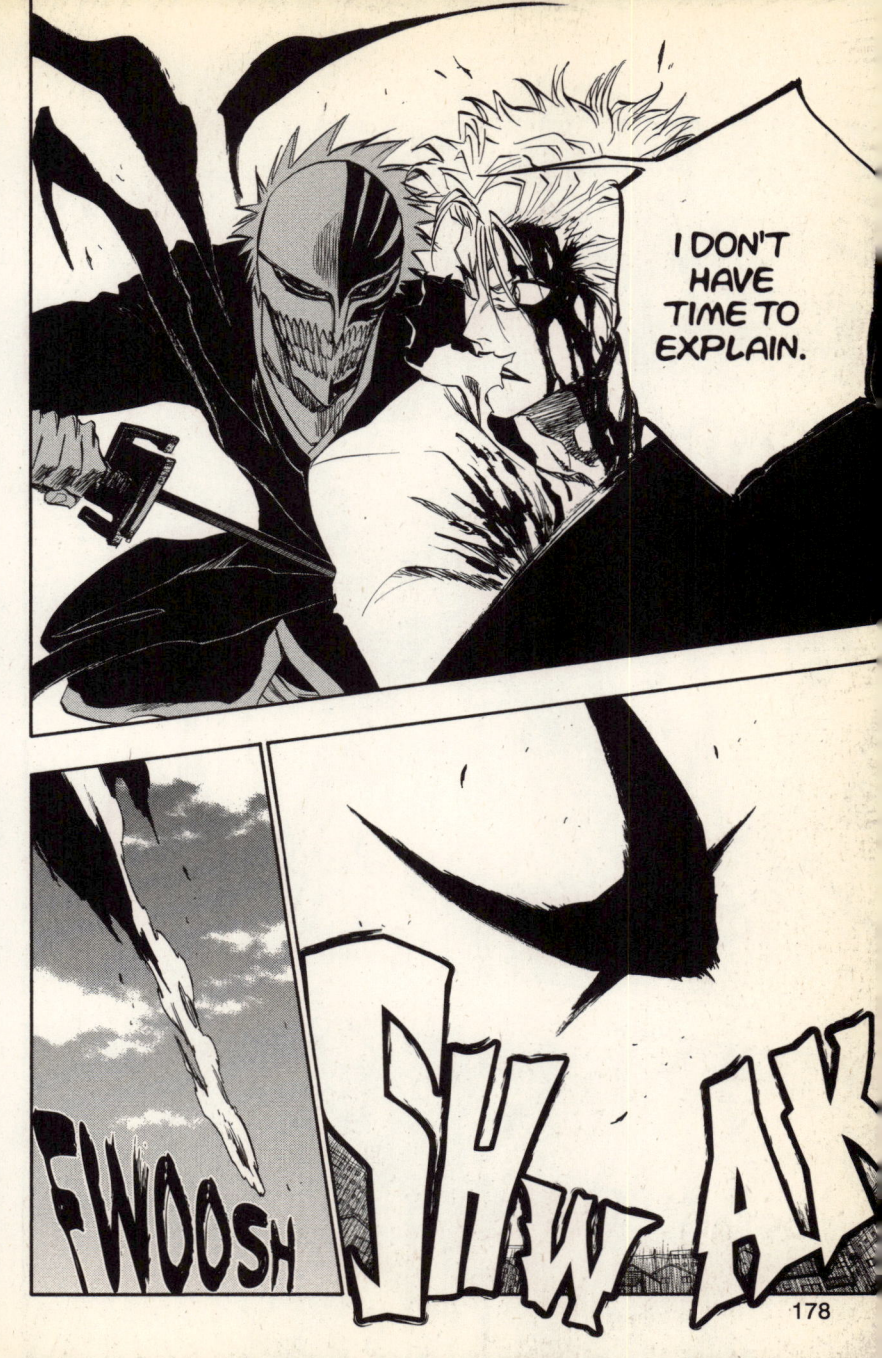

HOW DID YOU DO IT...
...IN ONLY A MONTH?!
FWIK
SHOOM
WHAM
I TOLD YOU...

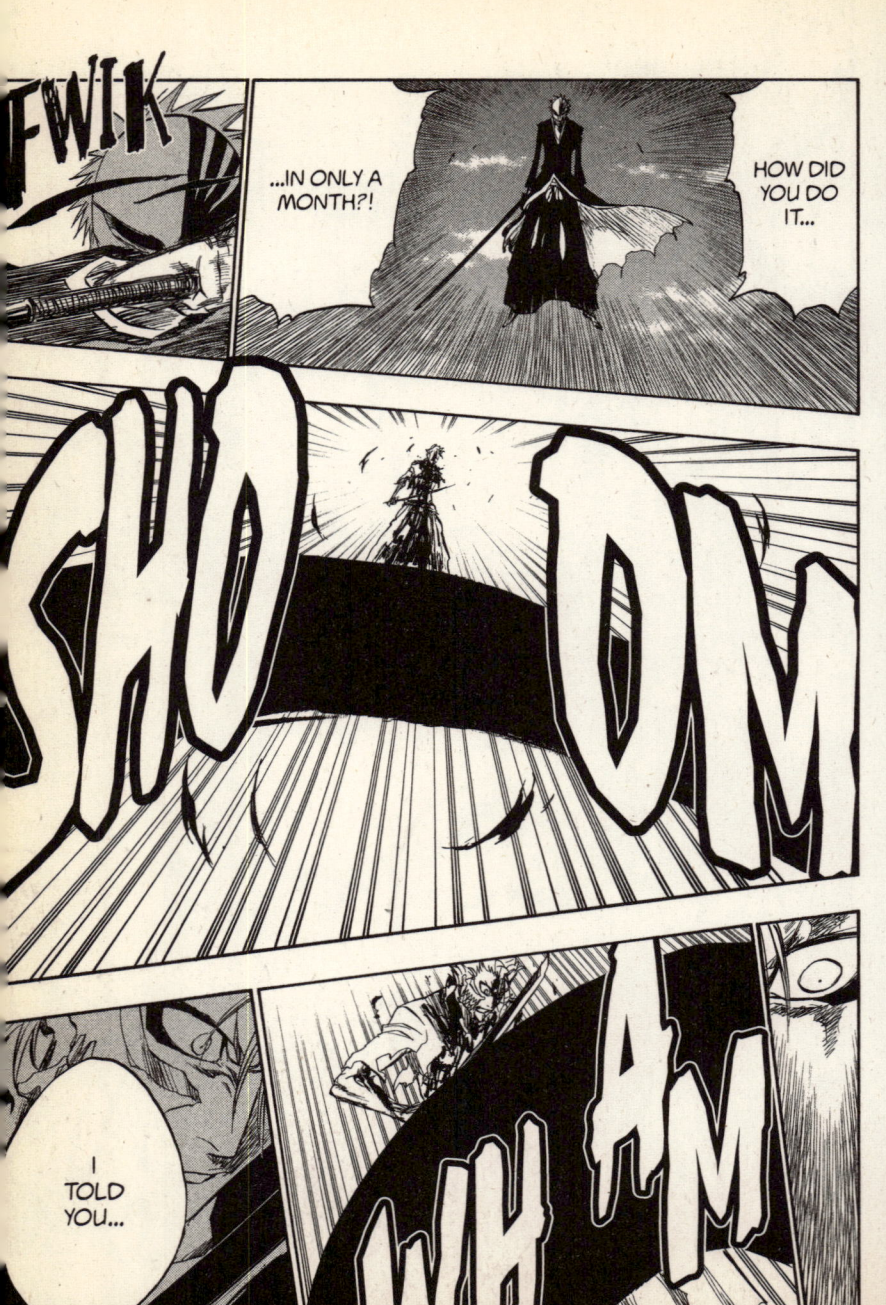

DOOOM
HUFF
HUFF
HUFF
THIS...
...ISN'T...
...SOUL REAPER POWER.
HOW?

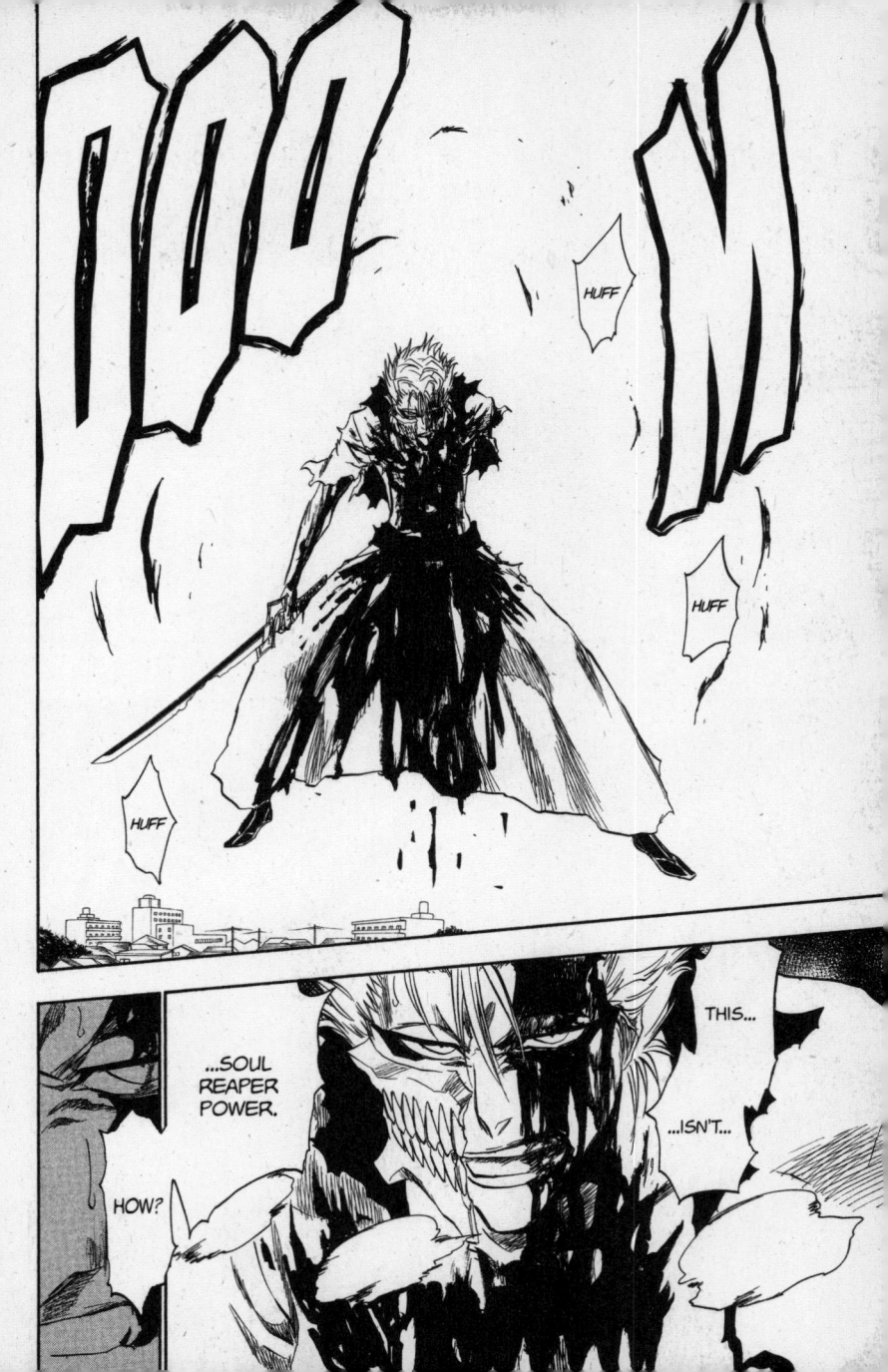

OH.
SORRY.
I MEAN...
...FOUR AGAINST EIGHT.
THWOOSH
SHWOOOOOO

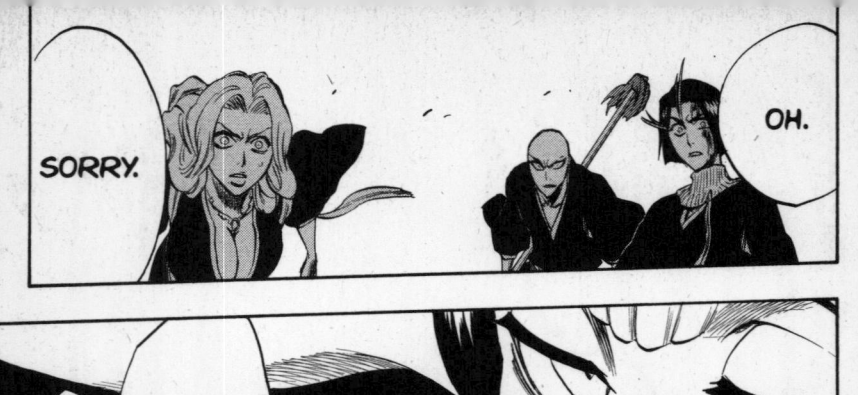

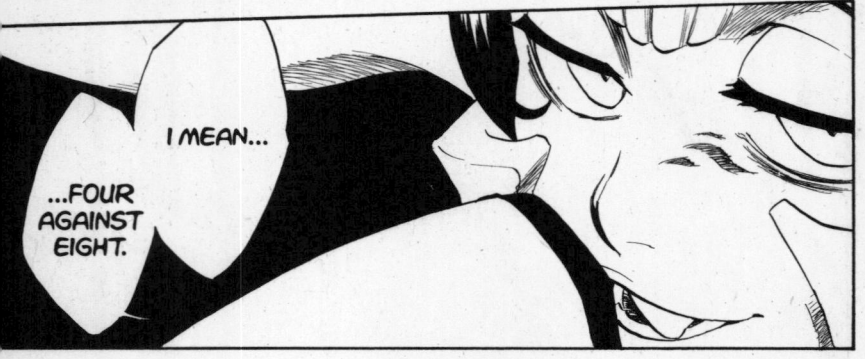

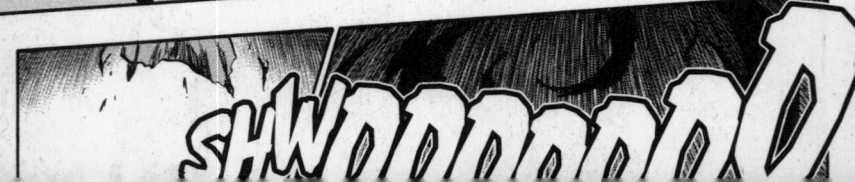

CAPTAIN!!

SEE?

DARN...

...IT.

I TOLD YOU TO FIGHT ME FOUR AGAINST ONE!

READ THIS WAY
EIGHT...
...TIMES?

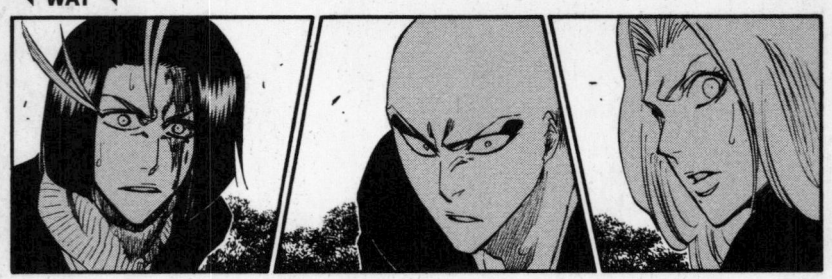

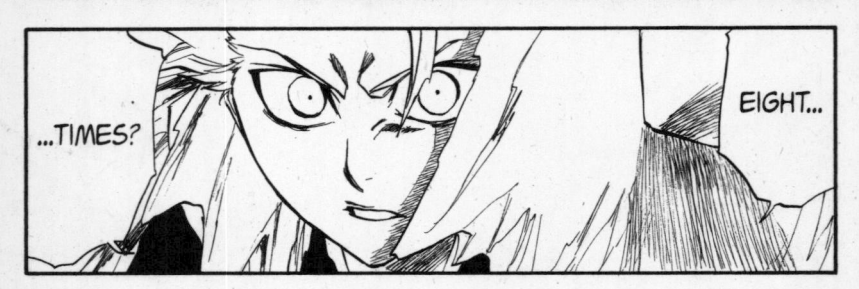

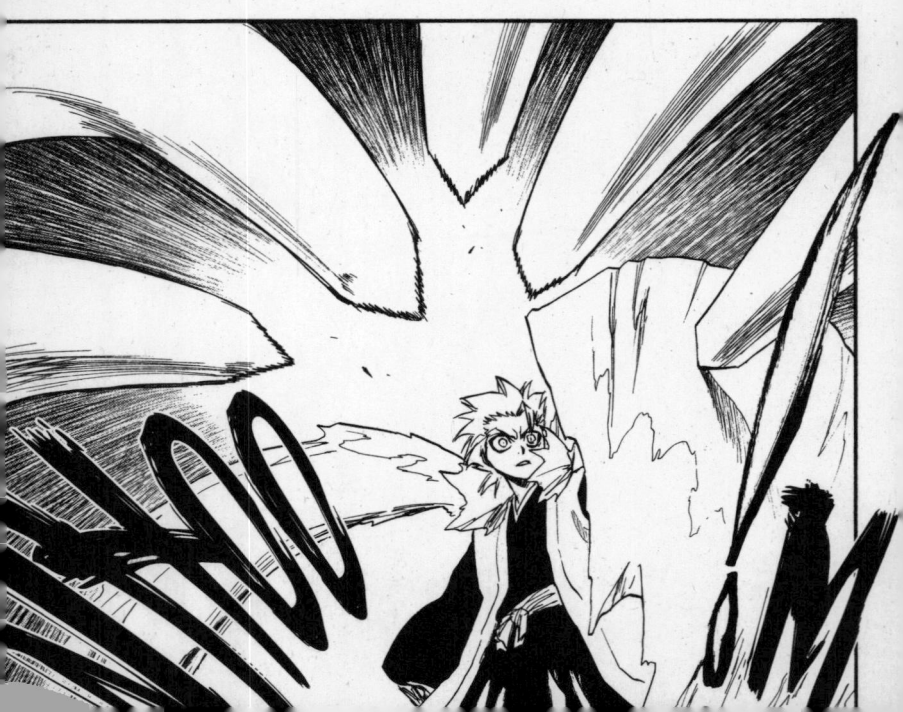

BOOM

...WERE EIGHT TIMES STRONGER?

SKRSHHHHHH
WHAT'S WRONG? IS THAT IT?
THAT'S YOUR RELEASE ATTACK?
HA HA!
GOOD JOB!
I REALLY DIDN'T THINK YOU COULD STOP IT.
YOU SURPRISED ME!
YOU CAPTAINS AREN'T TOO SHABBY.
BUT...
WHAT IF THAT ATTACK...

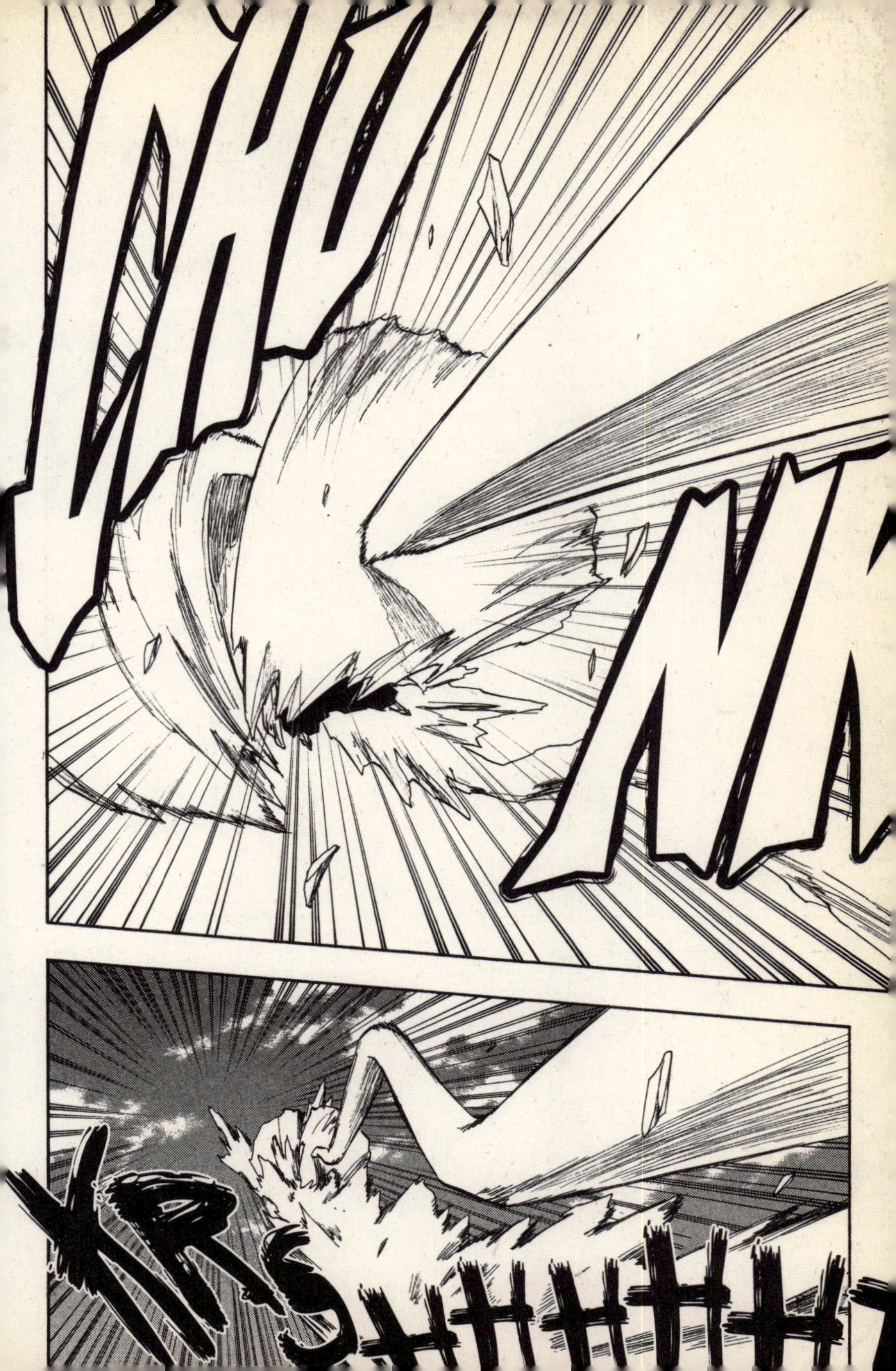
KRSHHHHHH

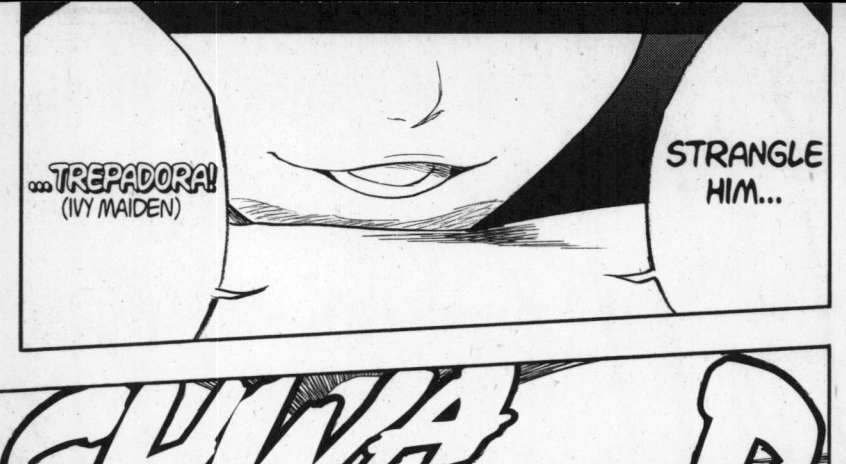

...TREPADORA!
(IVY MAIDEN)

STRANGLE HIM...

SHWAP!

HMPH!

KREKK

BANKAI!!

DAIGUREN HYÔRIN-MARU!!

SHH

RELEASE! ZANPAKU-TÔ...

I WON'T LET YOU!!

BLEACH
ブリーチ

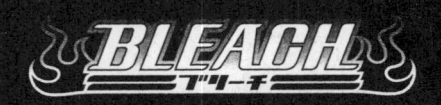

232. The Mascaron Drive 2

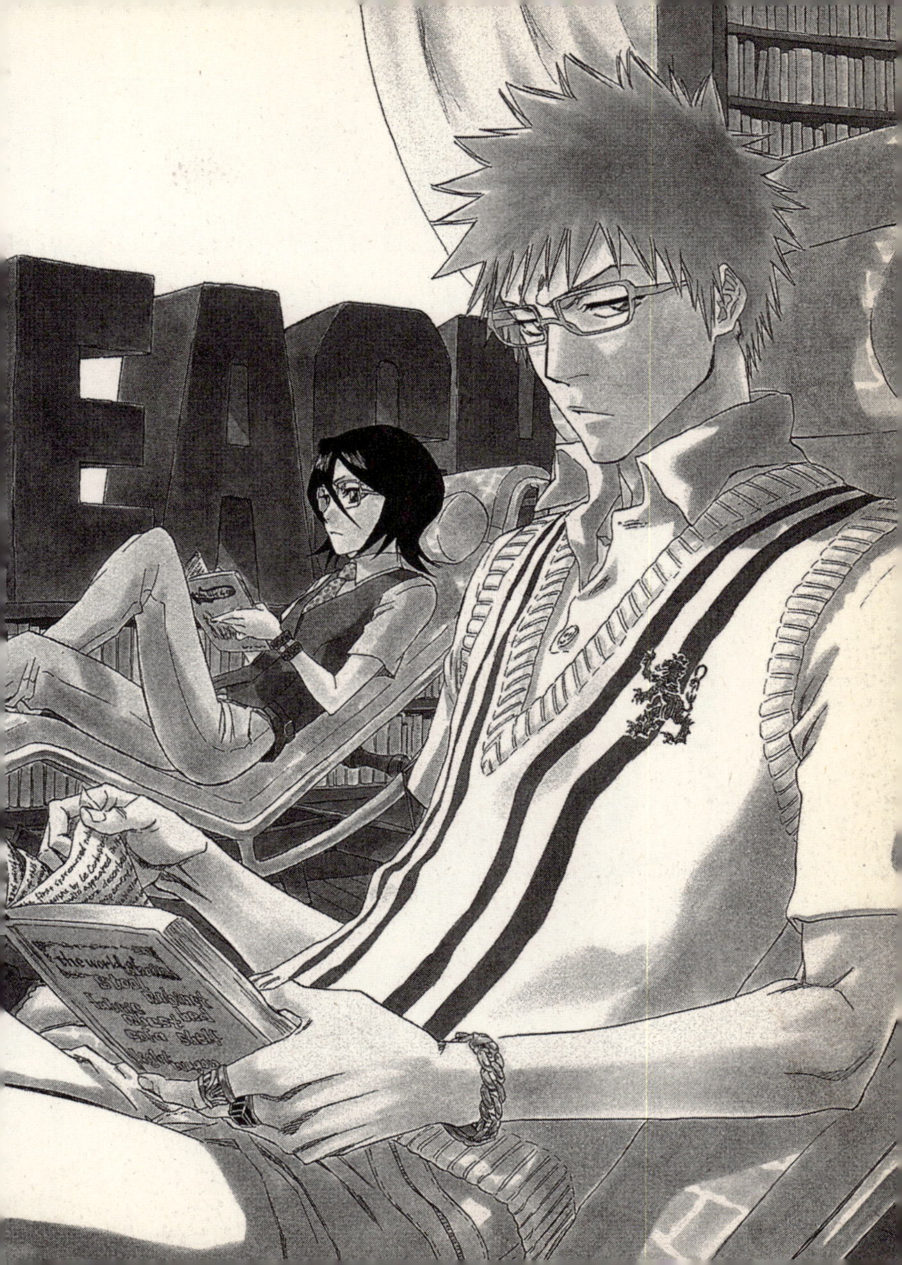
the world of

KLUNK

THAT'S RIGHT.

YES.

B... BUT...!

YOU'VE USED UP TOO MUCH ENERGY!

I'LL GO! YOU STAY HERE AND REST!!

AND...

BOTH OF YOU STAY HERE AND REST.

BUT YOU'RE NEARLY EXHAUSTED TOO, RENJI.

TMP

...I'LL GO.

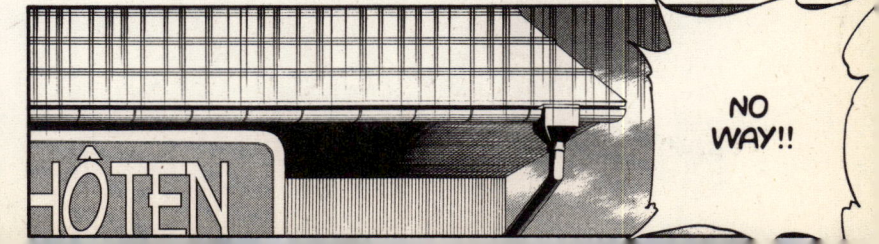

LET'S GO, FOUR ON ONE!

THESE GUYS ARE A JOKE.

I'LL RELEASE...

...AND TAKE YOU ALL ON.

SHUK

HÔTEN

NO WAY!!

SIIK

WOO

SHUT UP.

DON'T YOU GET IT?

SWOOOOOO

YOU CAN'T BEAT ME ONE ON ONE.

I TOLD YOU...

TWO AGAINST ONE ISN'T MY STYLE.

OR DO I HAVE TO KILL HIM?

WILL YOU TALK TO HIM?

CAN I HAVE THAT BOY?

YAMMY!

WHAT A PAIN...

NO?

HUA !!
WHAT WAS THAT ?!
IT WAS NICE AND COOL!
HMPH ...
LOOKS LIKE I'LL HAVE TO PERFORM BANKAI AGAINST HIM EVEN WITH THE GENTEI KAIJO LIFTED.

GETSUGA...

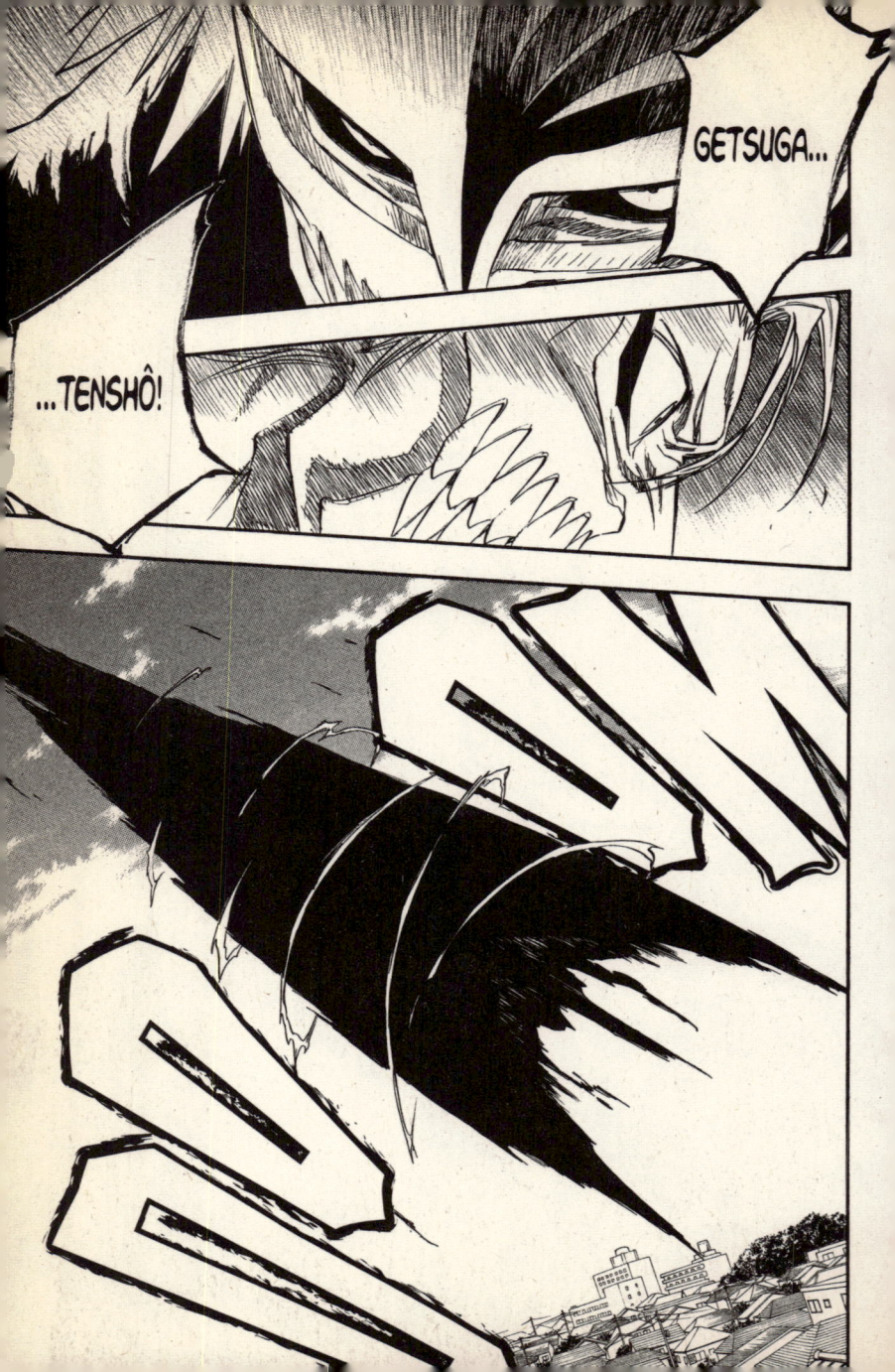

...TENSHÔ!

KRA

NE

SHRSHHHHW

UGH...

WOOOOOOOOOO
WHA...?
ZAK
ZAK
WHAT'S THAT?!
ZAK
SORRY, MAN.
I DON'T HAVE TIME TO EXPLAIN.
SHOOM
!

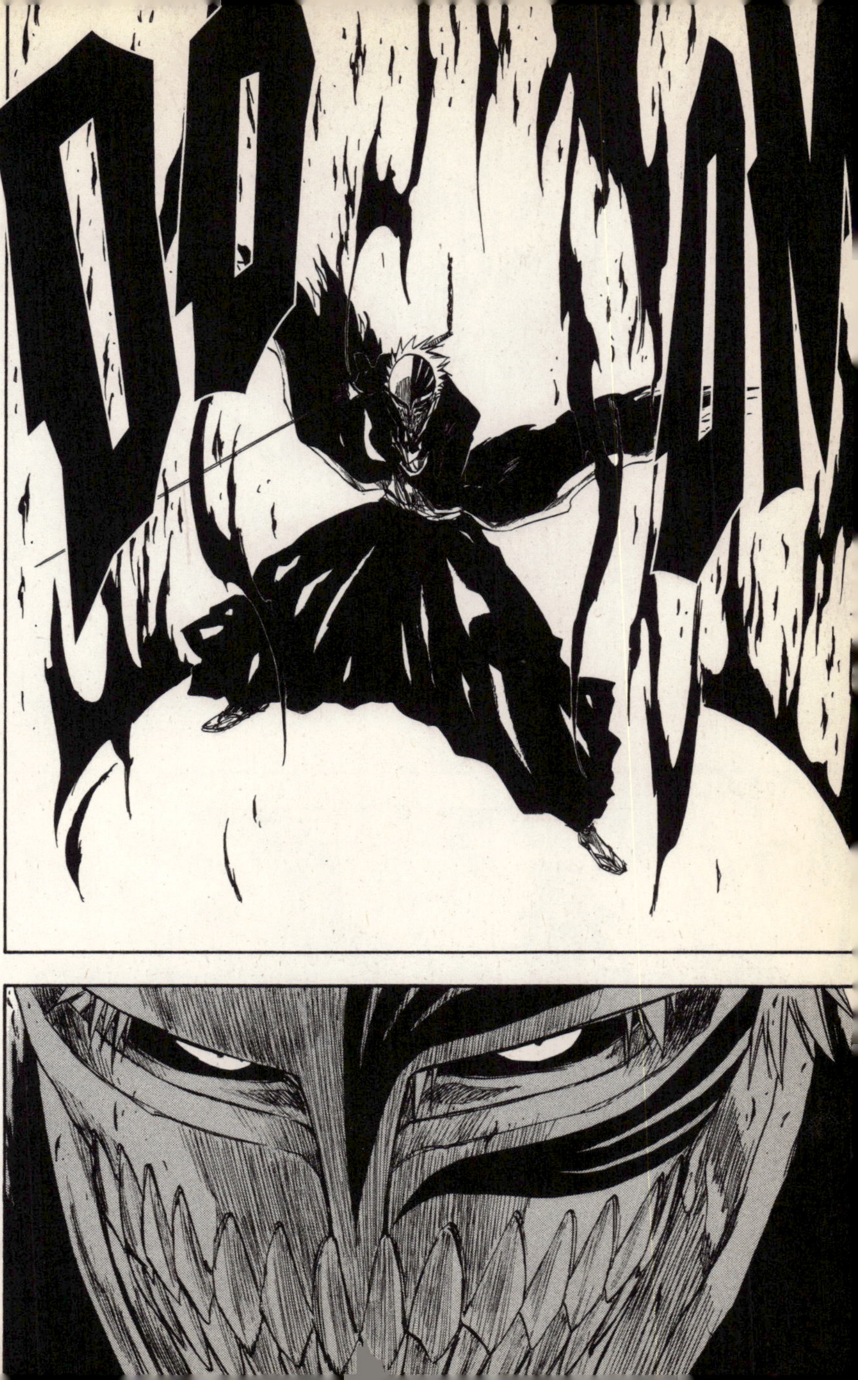

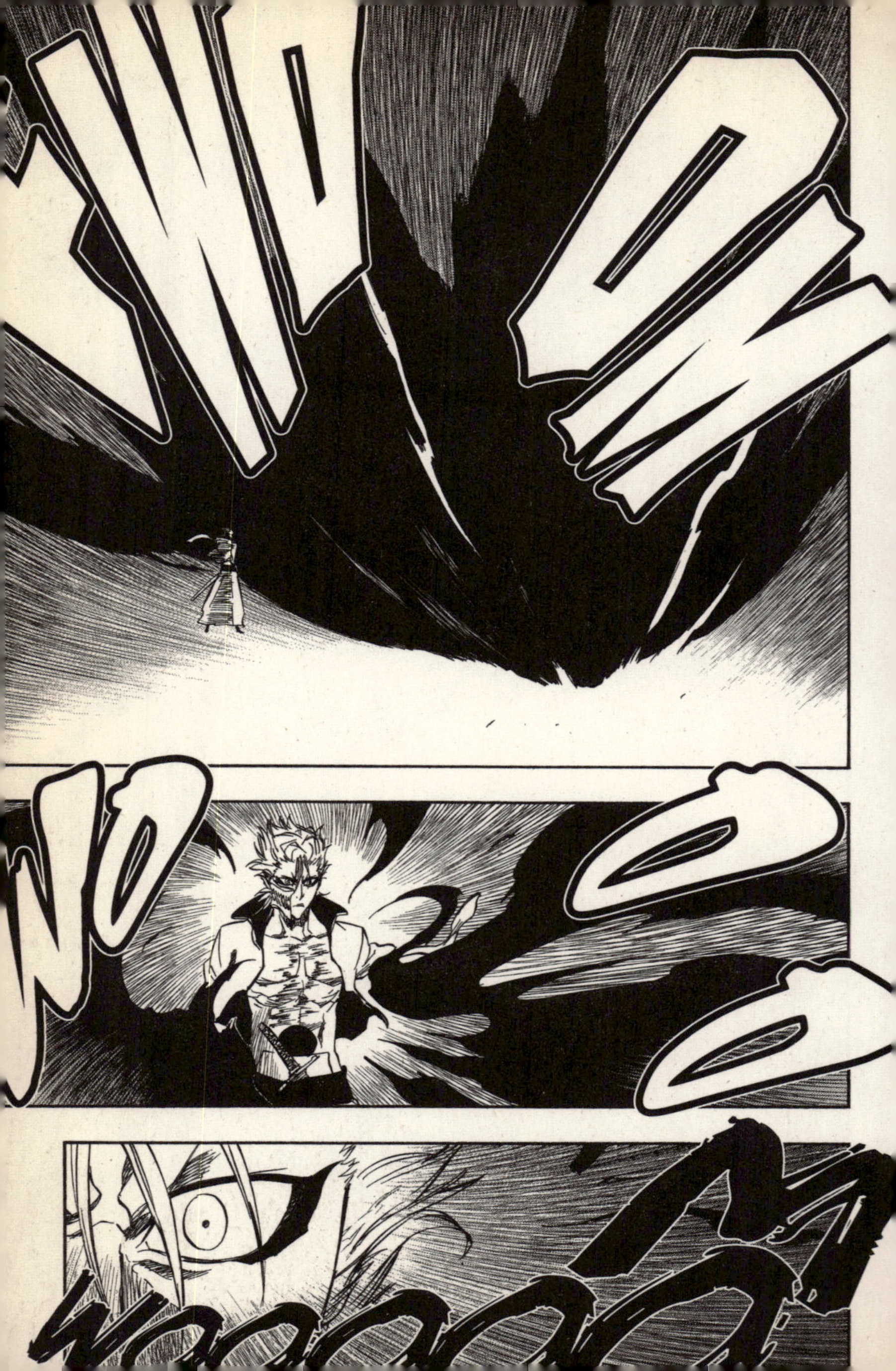

THEN I GUESS I DON'T HAVE TO...
...HOLD BACK!
IF YOU DO...
...YOU'RE GONNA DIE *REAL* QUICK.
WHUP
I CAN STAY HOLLOWFIED FOR EXACTLY ELEVEN SECONDS.
I'LL FINISH HIM BY THEN!

I'VE GOT A QUESTION FOR YOU...
... GRIMM-JOW.
RRMMM
RRRMMM
WHAT HAPPEN-ED...
...TO YOUR ARM?
I GOT RID OF IT.
I ONLY NEED ONE ARM...
...TO KILL YOU.
OH, YEAH?

RRMMMMMMMMMM
BANKAI, EH?
SO WHAT?
DID YOU FOR-GET?
YOUR BANKAI COULDN'T STOP ME.
MAYBE YOU FORGOT.
MY BANKAI ATTACK...
...GAVE YOU THAT SCAR!

HA!

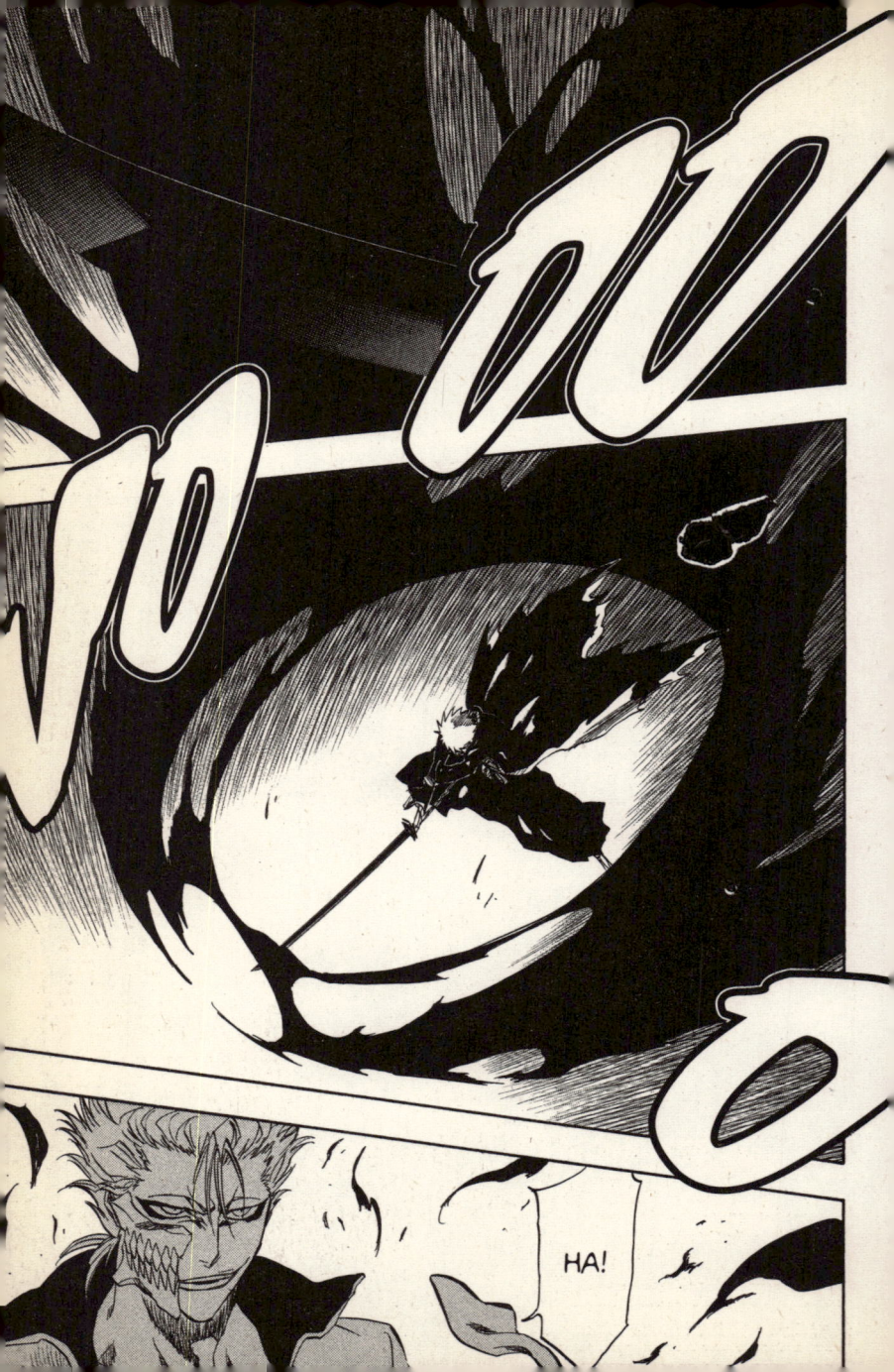

OKAY.

I'LL BE WAITING ON THE OTHER SIDE.

THIS ISN'T RIGHT. IT'S TOO SOON FOR THE ESPADAS TO SHOW UP!

THE HÔGYOKU WAS SUPPOSED TO AWAKEN IN THE WINTER!

WHAT'S...

...HAPPENING?!

READ THIS WAY

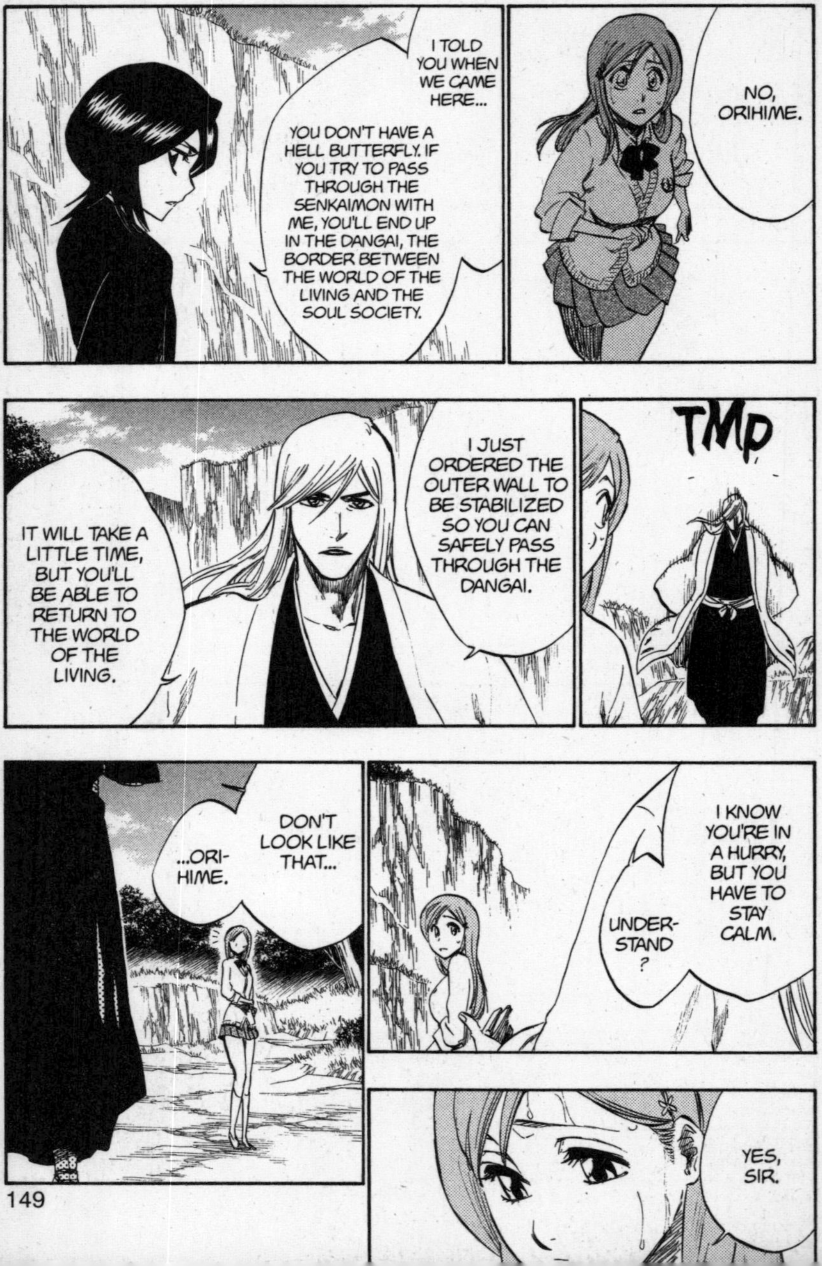

!

KU-CHIKI!

YES, SIR!

I JUST RECEIVED THE REPORT TOO.

THE KIDÔ CORPS ARE WORKING ON OPENING THE GATE!

GO TO THE SENKAI-MON IN FRONT OF THE BARRACKS!!

YES, SIR!

WAIT, RUKIA! I'LL GO WITH YOU!

DASH

RRMMMMMMMMM

FOUR ARRANCARS HAVE BEEN DETECTED IN NORTH KARAKURA.

RRMMMMMMMMM

THEY ARE BELIEVED TO BE ESPADAS!

THEY'RE ENGAGING THE HITSUGAYA ADVANCE TEAM!!

BLEACH 231. The Mascaron Drive

UWEEEEEEE!!!

231. The Mascaron Drive

RRMMMM

THE REACTION?!

WHAT COLOR IS IT?!

WHAT ABOUT THE GENTEI KAIJO*?!

IT'S BEEN AUTHORIZED!

TSU

I GOT IT!!

I GOT A REACTION!!

*RESTRICTION REMOVAL

IT'S VERMILION!!

THEY'RE ESPADAS!!

IT'S KINDA CUTE, BUT IT'S SO SMALL.
IT'S HARD TO FIND A NICE SWIMSUIT THAT FITS.
ISANE!!
TMP TMP TMP
I FOUND THE PERFECT BATHING SUIT...
SEXY!
...FOR YOU!!
K-KIYONE!
I CAN'T WEAR THAT!
HEY...
THAT'S NICE.

AND I'VE BEEN WAITING FOR YOU.

...HOW MUCH I'VE CHANGED...

...IN THE LAST MONTH.

I WANNA SHOW YOU...

I'VE BEEN LOOKING FOR YOU, SOUL REAPER.

HELLO.

LET HIM GO.

SHINJI!

ARE YOU NUTS?!

C'MON!

...CUT THAT ONE?

CAN I...

FWAP FWAP

...

LET GO OF ME!!

WELL THIS IS EXACTLY WHAT I'VE BEEN TRAINING FOR TOO!!

IT'S NOW OR NEVER!

THIS IS EXACTLY WHY YOUR PALS FROM THE SOUL SOCIETY ARE HERE!!

LET THEM HANDLE IT!!

YOU'RE NOT READY YET!!

WHAP

TEN!
THEN YOU'RE AN ESPADA.
YOU KNOW ABOUT US?
YOU MUST'VE FOUGHT SOMEBODY WITH A BIG MOUTH!
ARE YOU ...
...AN ESPADA TOO?
UH-HUH.
SHFF
MY NAME'S LUPPI.
I'M RANKED...
...NUMBER SIX--SEXTA.
AH...
FWAP FWAP FWAP

CAPTAIN TÔSHIRÔ HITSUGAYA, TENTH COMPANY!

WHAT A COINCI-DENCE! I'M A TEN TOO.
ARRAN-CAR DIEZ...
YAMMY!

ALL OF 'EM.

MA...

LET'S GO, ROOKIE!

DON'T JUST STAND THERE DROOLING!

HEY!

ANOTHER FREAK JOINS THE TEAM.

HMPH...

AH...

SHOOM

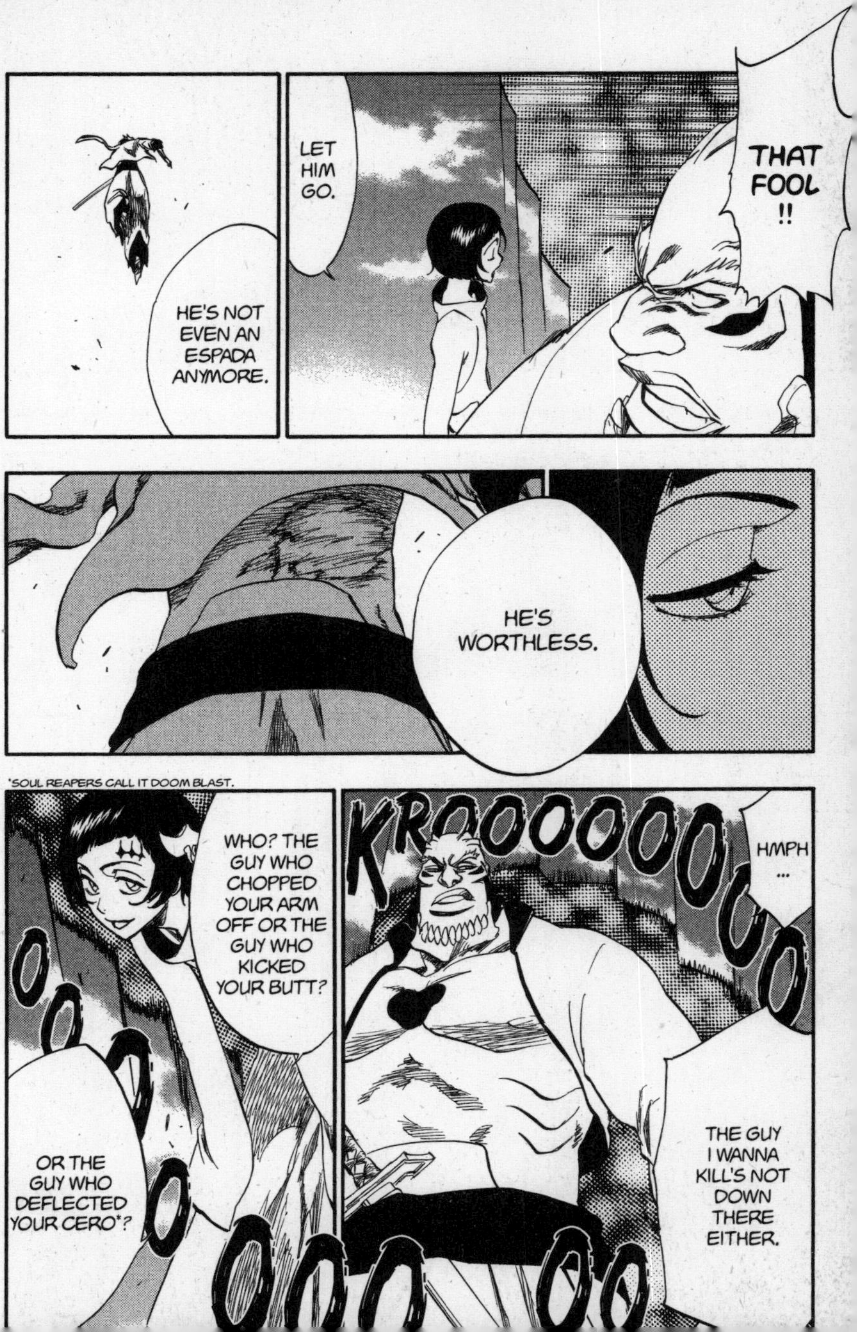

*SOUL REAPERS CALL IT DOOM BLAST.

READ THIS WAY

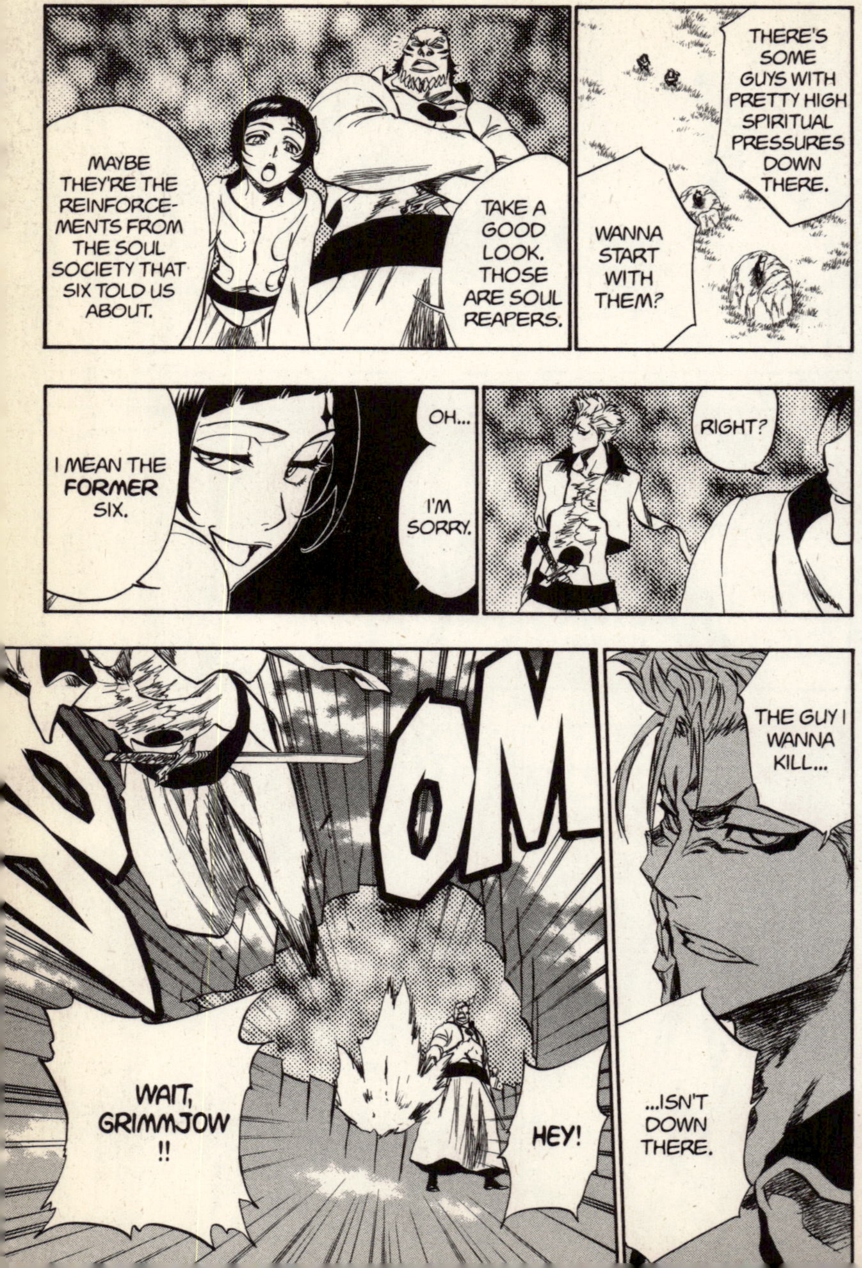

RRMMMMMMMMMM

BUT THERE'S NO TIME TO FIGURE OUT WHY.

THEY'RE DEFINITELY EARLY.

AREN'T THEY A LITTLE EARLY?!

ARRANCARS NOW?

HEY!

WE PICKED A GOOD SPOT.

SHW
BLEACH
ブリーチ
230. Dead White Invasion

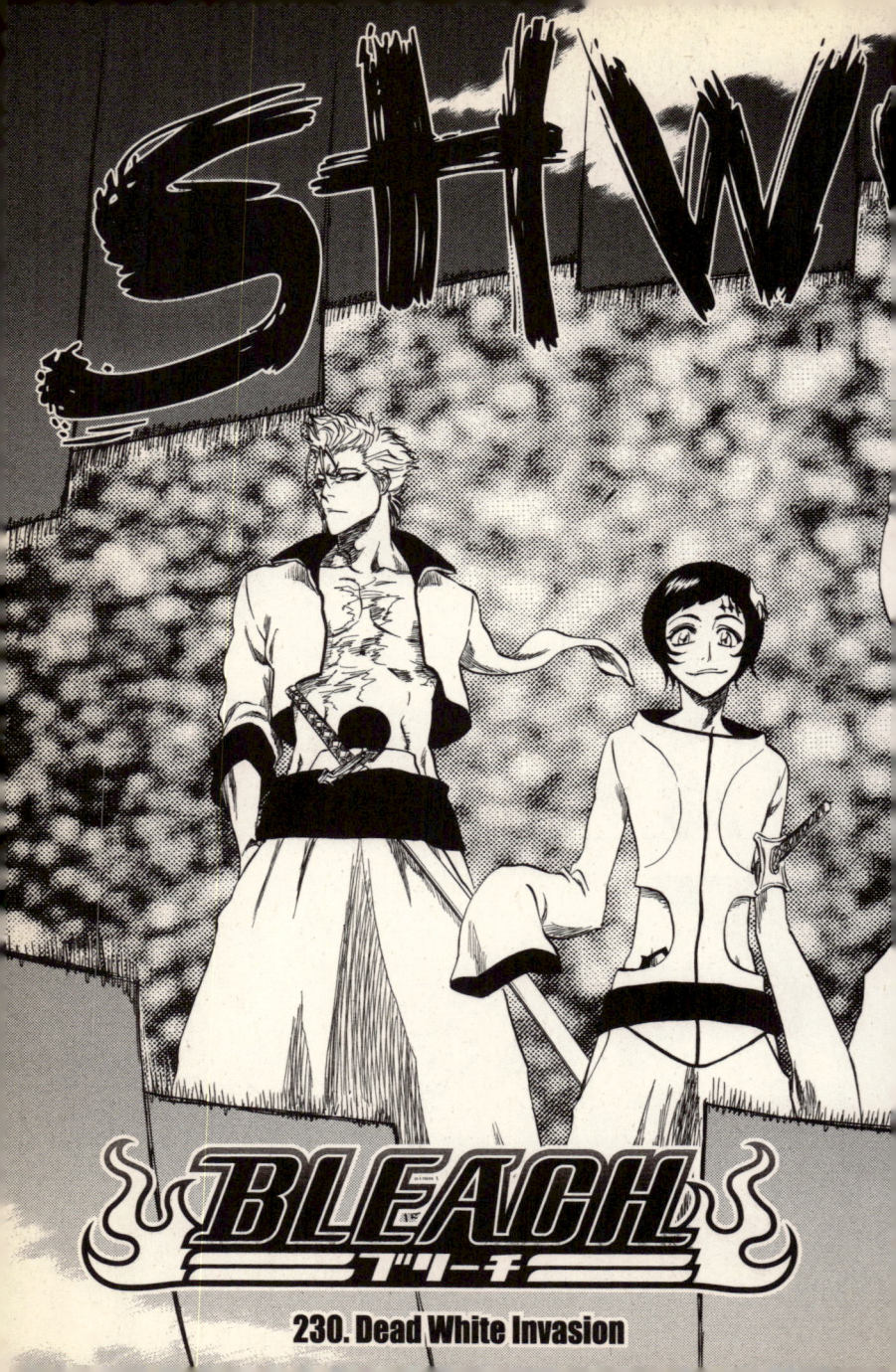

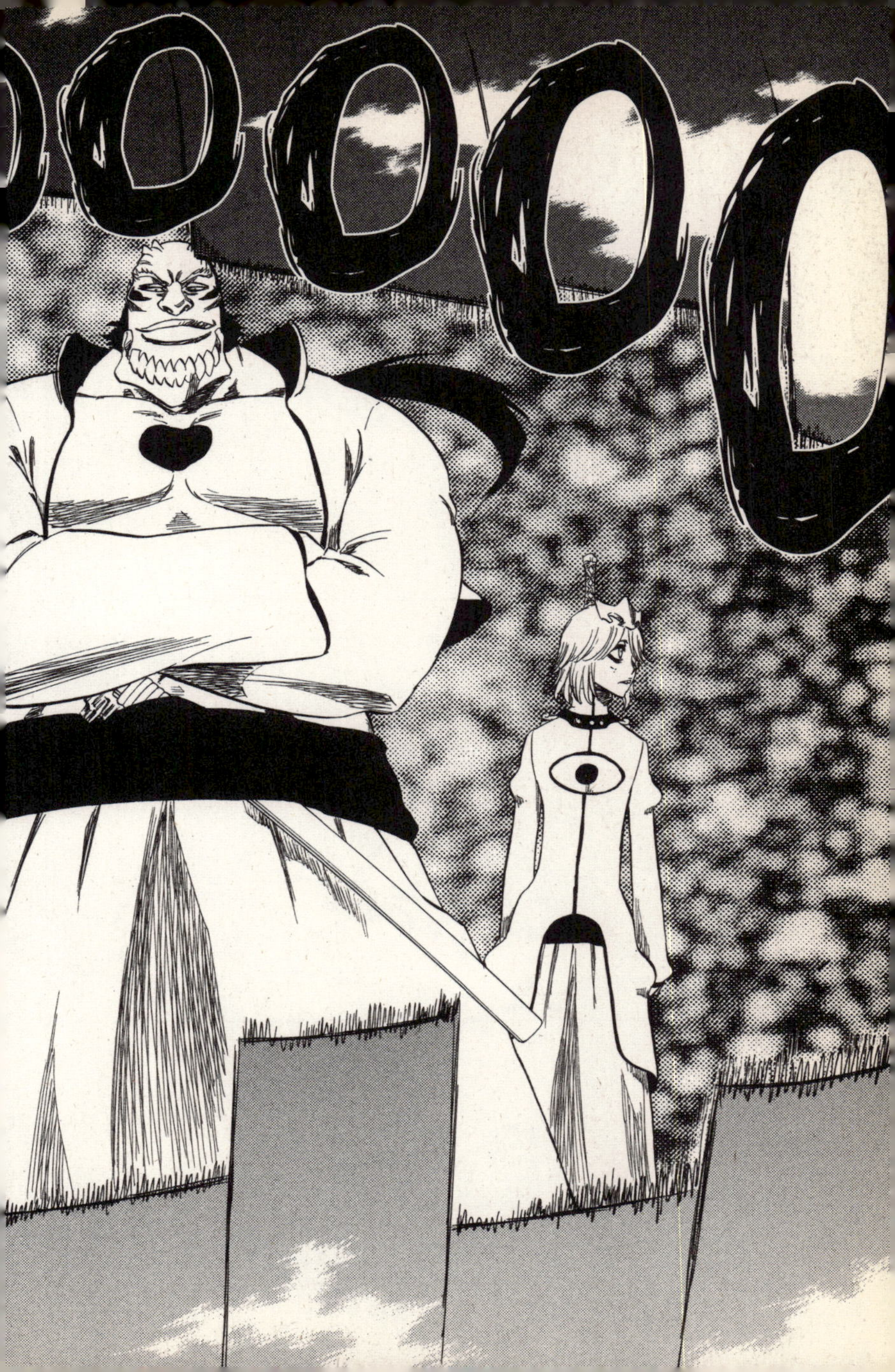
OOOOO

KRAK
SKREKK

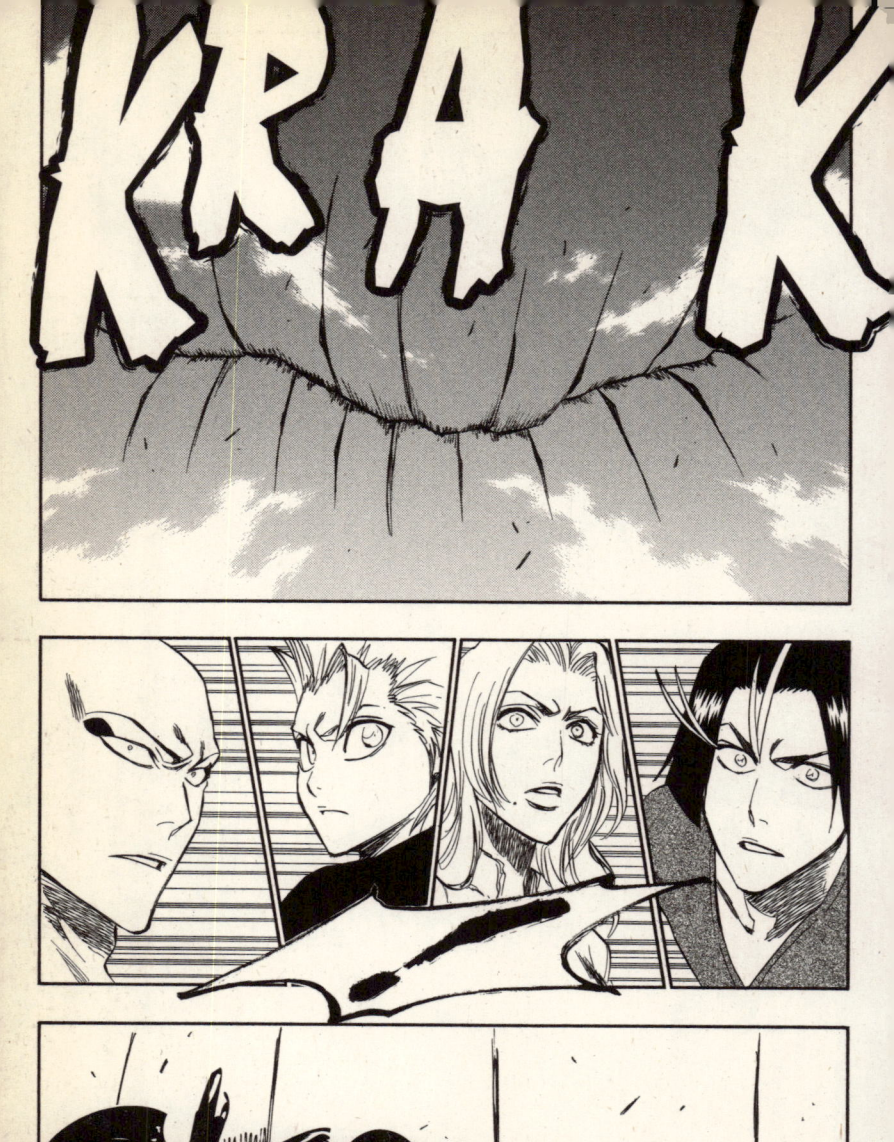

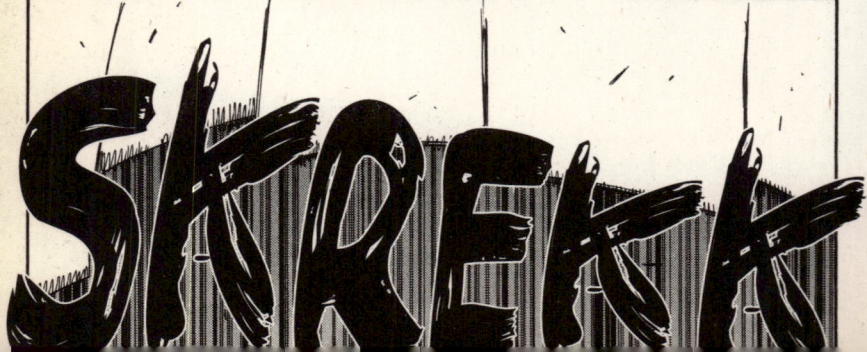

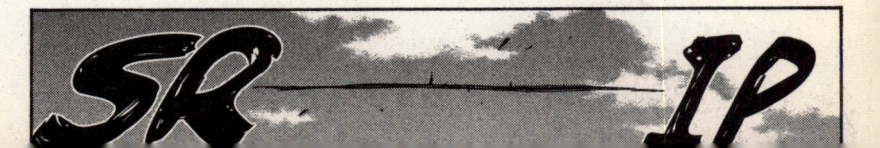

...MUCH LESS TO BUILD STRENGTH.

NOT MUCH TIME TO MEND THE HEART...

IF ONLY THIS FLEETING PEACE...

...COULD LAST A LITTLE LONGER...

SR IP

CAPTAIN TÔSEN NEVER ASKED US TO DO ANYTHING.	I NEVER REALIZED THAT A CAPTAIN'S DUTIES WERE SO DIFFICULT.

SORRY. I HAVE WORK TO DO.

STAY AWHILE.

I SHOULD BE GOING.

WELL...

MAYBE ANOTHER TIME.

THOUGH I WOULDN'T MIND WATCHING THOSE TWO TRAIN FOR A WHILE.

FOUR MONTHS, EH?

THOSE YOUNG PEOPLE ARE UNUSUAL. MAYBE THEY'LL BECOME SOUL REAPERS WHEN THEY REACH THE SOUL SOCIETY.

AND YOU KNOW...

EVEN THOUGH THEY LIVE IN DIFFERENT WORLDS...

...FRIENDSHIP IS A FINE THING.

NO. THIS IS GOOD.

OH! THAT'S RIGHT.

SO, WHAT DID YOU COME HERE FOR?

WAS THERE SOMETHING YOU WANTED?

ELEVENTH COMPANY'S CAPTAIN WON'T WAKE UP AND I DON'T KNOW WHERE THE ASSISTANT CAPTAIN IS.

AND THOSE TWO FROM TWELFTH COMPANY WON'T COME OUT OF THE LAB.

IT'S CHAOS AROUND HERE. TENTH COMPANY'S IN THE WORLD OF THE LIVING AND...

WHAT ARE YOU DOING WITH THIS?

THIS MONTH'S SEIREITEI BULLETIN...

THE MAIL-ORDER CATALOGUE'S INSIDE.

I WAS SURPRISED WHEN SHE SHOWED UP WITH THAT DESPERATE LOOK AND ASKED ME TO OPEN THE TRAINING GROUNDS BEHIND THE BARRACKS.
SIP
SHE'S FOUND HERSELF A FRIEND.
I'M HAPPY FOR HER.
FORGIVE ME.
DON'T SAY THAT.
EVEN IF THAT FRIEND...
...IS A HUMAN?

THAT'S KUCHIKI AND ONE OF THE RYOKA...

ER...

THEY'VE BEEN AT IT A MONTH.

THEY'RE TRAINING FOR THE COMING WAR.

ORIHIME.

RUKIA WAS NEVER GOOD AT MAKING FRIENDS.

SHE...

...RARELY OPENS UP.

HEY! YOU THINK SO TOO?

THEY LOOK...

...LIKE THEY'RE HAVING TOO MUCH FUN.

The Seireitei
HMM...
Training Grounds Behind Thirteenth Company's Barracks
THERE YOU ARE.
WHAT ARE YOU DOING?

230. Dead White Invasion

OH...
HELLO, SHÛHEI.
I WAS JUST...
...TAKING A BREAK AND ENJOYING THE SHOW.

THIS ?!
PINK LAMÉ
ONE-PIECE
BUT WAIT! HOW CAN MS. YORUICHI BE WRONG?!
WHAT?! IT'S HIDEOUS! IT LOOKS LIKE A LITTLE GIRL'S SWIMSUIT!
BUT...AM I OKAY WITH THAT?! I KNOW IT'S MS. YORUICHI, BUT PERHAPS I HAVE TO VOICE AN OPINION SOMETIMES.
MS. YORU-ICHI!
I PREFER THIS YELLOW ONE...
THANK YOU!

READ THIS WAY
HUH?
YOU SAY SOMETHING, IKKAKU?
NO.
IT'S NOTHING.
KRAK

OR I'LL SEND YOU BACK TO THE SOUL SOCIETY!!

SHUT UP AND CONCENTRATE!!

WHAM
THWAK
AAAH
THWAM

CAN'T THEY TALK TO THEIR SWORDS MORE QUIETLY?

GEEZ...

THE CLOUD'S ARE MOVING...

...

KLANK KLANK KLANK

CRAP! CRAP! CRAP!

BREAK! BREAK!! BREAK, DARN IT!!

CRAP!!

DARN YOU!!

AAAAAAAH!!! GRAAAAAAAAAA

I DON'T THINK I CAN EVER EXTERIORIZE THIS CREEP!!

ACTUALLY, I WOULDN'T DO IT EVEN IF HE BEGGED ME TO!!

FUJIKUJAKU'S TICKING ME OFF!!

HE'S SO SNOBBY AND BOSSY AND THINKS HE'S THE BEST-LOOKING GUY IN THE WORLD!! I HATE HIM!!

WHAT'S WRONG WITH YOU?!

SHUT UP.

RAAAH!! I HATE YOU!!

WOOSH THWAK

THAT'S YOU TO A "T".

I BET YOU SEE PICTURES OF YOURSELF AND SAY, "I DON'T LOOK LIKE THAT!!"

NOW MY HAINEKO'S A STUPID, NEEDY, MOODY SLOB.

WE'RE TOTAL OPPOSITES.

WHAT ARE YOU TALKING ABOUT?

HE'S JUST LIKE YOU.

...GRIMM-JOW?

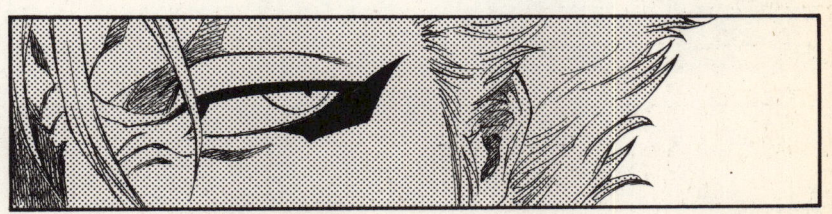

SHWUFF

YES.
CARRY IT OUT.
THE CHOICE IS YOURS.
TAKE WHOMEVER YOU LIKE.
YES, SIR.
KLAK
OH, AND...
WOULD YOU...
...LIKE TO GO TOO...

WONDERWEISS...

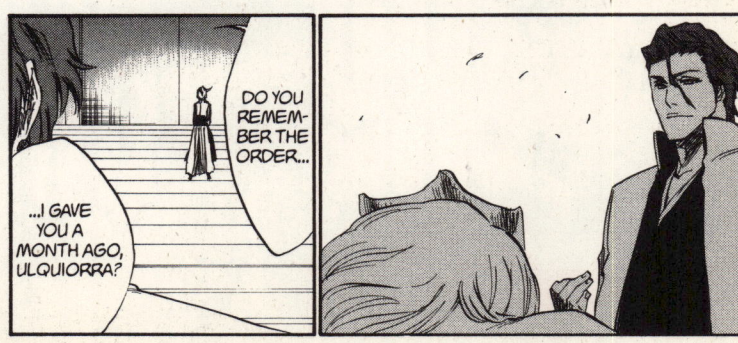

WONDERWEISS...

MARGERA.

DO YOU REMEMBER THE ORDER...

...I GAVE YOU A MONTH AGO, ULQUIORRA?

WHEN THE HÔGYOKU, IN A DORMANT STATE WITH ITS SEAL REMOVED...
KREEK
SWUP
...IS JOINED WITH SOME-ONE WHO POSSESSES TWICE THE SPIRIT ENERGY OF A CAPTAIN...
...FOR A SHORT TIME...
...ITS FULL POWER...
...IS RELEASED.
BOOM
KREESH
CAN YOU...
...TELL ME YOUR NAME...
...NEW COMRADE?

PLUMP

HWOOOOOO

"What's the status of the Hôgyoku?"

"It's at 50 percent."

"It will awaken... exactly when the Soul Society expects it to."

"But there's a secret... that only those who've actually touched the Hôgyoku know."

"I doubt... that even Kisuke Urahara... who developed it and sealed it away so abruptly... and never removed the seal, would know it."

...WON'T BE LONG NOW.

IT...

KLAK

KREEK

ULQUIORRA...
...ENTERING.

...ULQUIORRA...
...AND YAMMY.

WELCOME...

SO LITTLE TIME...
WE HAVE TO HURRY.
KLAK
TOMP
KLAK
TOMP
TOMP
KLAK
TOMP
KLAK
TOMP
KLAK

IT'S COOL, MAN.
I BORROW IT MYSELF EVERY COUPLE OF DAYS.
I'M NOT LIKE YOU!!
I LOOK AT IT TWICE A DAY.
YEAH, I KNOW !!
BUT I'M NOT A PERV LIKE YOU, ALL RIGHT?!
I'M NOT A PERV!
I'M JUST REALLY CURIOUS!!
SO ARE MOST PERVERTS.
WHAT ABOUT YOU?! YOU'RE CURIOUS TOO!
...
A LITTLE OVER TEN SECONDS AFTER ONE MONTH...
I GUESS IT'S GOING TO TAKE TIME.
THE HÔGYOKU WAKES AT THE END OF DECEMBER...
WE'VE GOT TWO MORE MONTHS.

CHOW TIME!!

GET YOUR BUTTS OVER HERE!!

LAST ONE IN LINE HAS TO DO THE DISHES!!

OOH!

SO?

HOW'S ICHIGO'S TRAINING GOING, HIYORI?

WEREN'T YOU WATCHING?

HE'S ONLY UP TO A LITTLE OVER TEN SECONDS.

BALDY'S A JOKE.

IT'S NOT GOING ANYWHERE.

HE'S DOG MEAT.

YOU LITTLE...

MAYBE HE JUST DOESN'T HAVE WHAT IT TAKES?

SHUT UP, PERVERT!!

YOU'RE NOT EVEN INVOLVED IN THE TRAINING SO KEEP YOUR MOUTH SHUT!

JUST GIVE UP.

I LENT YOU THAT GIRLIE MAGAZINE THE OTHER DAY, REMEMBER?!

YES I AM, MORON!!

STOP TELLING LIES THAT SOUND KINDA TRUE!!

I DIDN'T BORROW ANYTHING FROM YOU!!

"YOU'RE ALREADY DEAD."
FWUMP
THAT'S SUCH A DEEP LINE, HUH?
HE'S TELLING THESE GUYS THEY'RE DEAD...
...BUT THEY JUST DON'T REALIZE IT YET.
DON'T YOU SEE?
YOU'RE ALIVE AND THEY'RE DEAD...
THWAM
THWAM
JUST LIKE THAT.
IS THAT SUPPOSED TO SOUND LIKE WHAT SCHIELE* SAID OR SOME-THING?
AND WILL YOU STOP READING MY COMICS BEFORE I DO? YOU SPOIL EVERY-THING?
KR
EESH
GET UP, FOOL!!
DO YOU KNOW HOW MANY TIMES I COULD'VE KILLED YOU?!
OH, I GET IT!
YOU THOUGHT SOUL REAPERS WERE SUPPOSED TO GET KILLED A LOT, RIGHT?!
WELL YOU'RE WRONG, BALDY!!
KLAK
SHUT...
...UP!
KLANK

*Egon Schiele. A German Expressionist painter who said: "Everything is dead while it lives."

MASTER AIZEN WANTS TO SEE US.

BLEACH

229. The Howling Tempest

BO OM

October 29, Karakura: Underground Headquarters of the Vizards

READ THIS WAY
SPLAK
FWSHHH
FWUP
IT'S NO GOOD.
THAT WOULD'VE SPLIT HER IN TWO IF I WAS AT MY BEST.
SPLAT
STU-PID.
LET'S GO.
TMP
WHERE ARE WE GOING?

MAYBE.
THE TREATMENT ...
...IS COMPLETE.
HOW IS IT, SIR?
GOOD.
WHUP
WHUP
IS THERE ANY LOSS OF MOBILITY OR SENSITIVITY COMPARED TO BEFORE THE DISMEMBERMENT?
HUH?

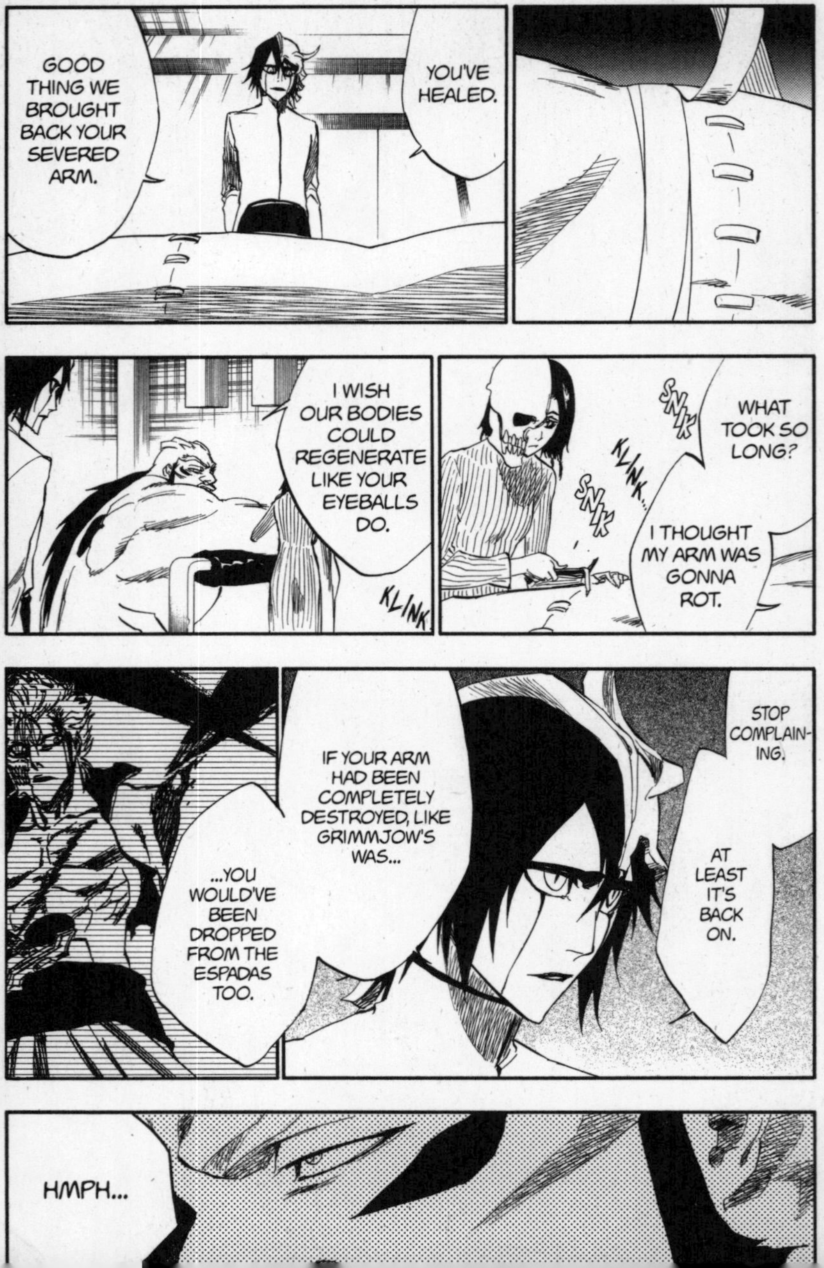

KREEEEK

"IS THAT YOU, ULQUIORRA?"

"..."

"WHAT DO YOU WANT?"

229. The Howling Tempest

KLAK
KLAK
KLAK
KREEK

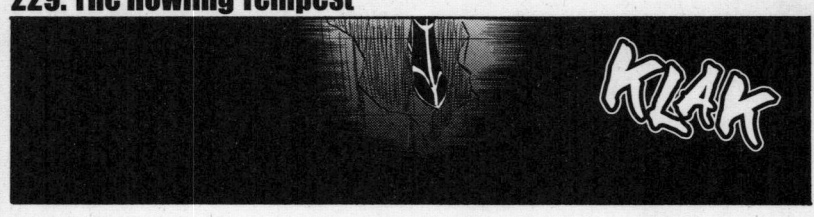

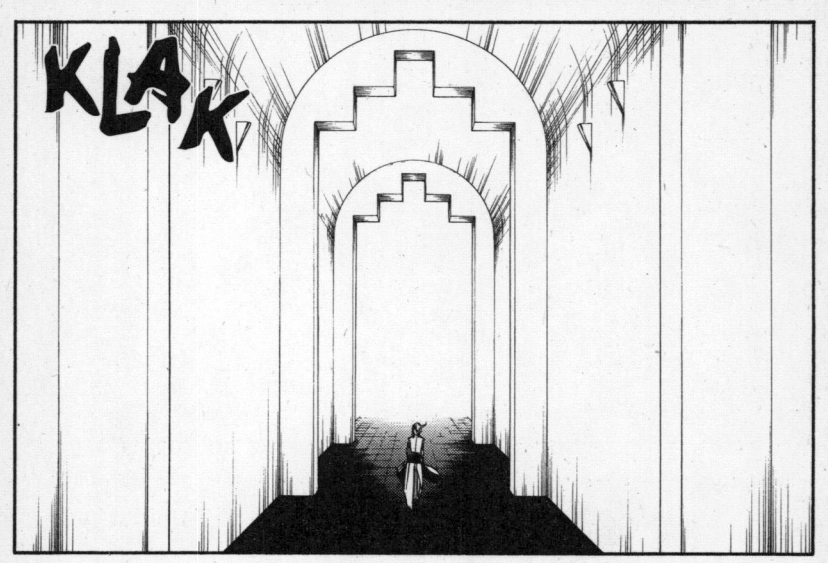

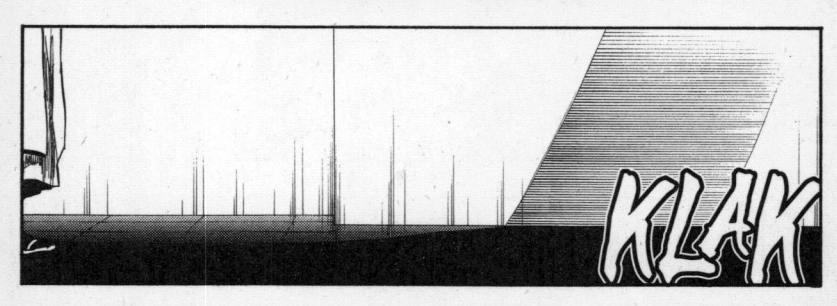

HMM... I'M GOING WITH THIS ONE!
OH! EXCELLENT CHOICE!
YOU LOOK SO ELEGANT PICKING OUT A SWIM-SUIT!!
GASP
WHAT AM I DOING?! I NEED TO GET ONE FOR ME!
SOI FON!
I FOUND ONE FOR YOU TOO!

LET'S GO...

...ORI-HIME.

ICHIGO...

I'M WEAK, SO I ALWAYS TURN TO YOU.

BUT I WON'T TURN TO YOU THIS TIME.

THE NEXT TIME WE SEE EACH OTHER...

...I'LL BE ABLE TO FIGHT WITHOUT LOOKING AT YOUR BACK.

YEAH.

LET'S GO, RUKIA.

RUKIA!

AS LONG AS HE'S SAFE...

...THAT'S ENOUGH FOR ME.

I CAME HERE BECAUSE I SENSED A TRACE OF ICHIGO'S SPIRITUAL PRESSURE.

IF HE HASN'T TOLD ME ABOUT THIS, I'M SURE THERE'S A GOOD REASON.

DON'T TELL ME.

I DON'T WANT TO KNOW.

UM...

YOU SEE, RUKIA?!

INSIDE THERE'S A~

...THE IMPORTANT THING ISN'T HOW YOU **SHOULD** BE...

...BUT HOW YOU **WANT** TO BE.

THANK YOU!

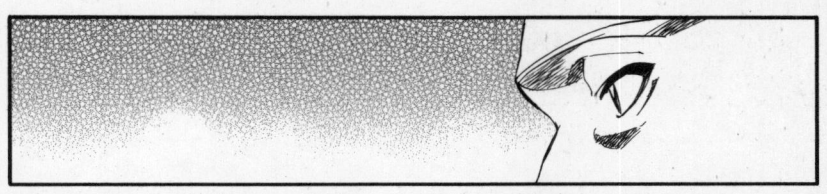

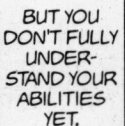

YES.

I WANT TO FIGHT!

THERE IS A WAY FOR YOU TO FIGHT, BUT YOU MUST FIND IT.

BUT YOU DON'T FULLY UNDER-STAND YOUR ABILITIES YET.

THEN YOU SHALL.

PLEASE REMEMBER THIS...

ORI-HIME...

NOW THAT TSUBAKI'S FIXED...

...YOU SHOULD BE ABLE TO JOIN THE BATTLE LINE.

BUT I...

...WOULD ADVISE YOU NOT TO.

DO YOU STILL...

...WANT TO FIGHT?

IF YOUR ABILITY IS LIKE MINE...

...YOU'RE NOT SUITED FOR COMBAT...

...ESPECIALLY AGAINST THE ARRANCARS.

POP
HUH?
WHAT, WOMAN?
YOU SHOULD SEE YOURSELF RIGHT NOW!
TSUBAKI, YOU'RE BACK!! YAY!!
WHOA!!
WHAT THE?! HEY! LET GO!!
SHUKASHUKASHUKA
THANK YOU, MR. HACHI!!

FOR HACHI...
...AND PROBABLY OTHERS, AS WELL.
I SEE.
IT GOT BROKEN INTO SO MANY PIECES THAT YOU COULDN'T FIX IT...
SO THEY SAID YOU COULDN'T FIGHT.
UM...
NOT EXACTLY, BUT I'VE EXPLAINED IT FIVE TIMES ALREADY SO THAT'S CLOSE ENOUGH.
IS THAT RIGHT?
BUT IT'S STRANGE.
AS FAR AS I CAN TELL, YOU POSSESS AN ABILITY VERY MUCH LIKE MY OWN.
IF SO, YOU SHOULD BE ABLE TO...
...RESTORE THESE BROKEN PIECES WITH EASE.
KEEEEEEEE

I DON'T GET IT!

I THINK HE'S HAPPY.

STOP WHINING!!
MAKE HER GO AWAY!!
WHO IS THAT GIRL ANYWAY?! I DON'T LIKE HER!!
WHY'S HACHI FIXING HER WEAPON?!

IT PROBABLY...

WE...
...RARELY MEET ANYONE WITH OUR SAME ABILITIES.

...FEELS LIKE FINDING A LONG-LOST RELATIVE.

READ THIS WAY

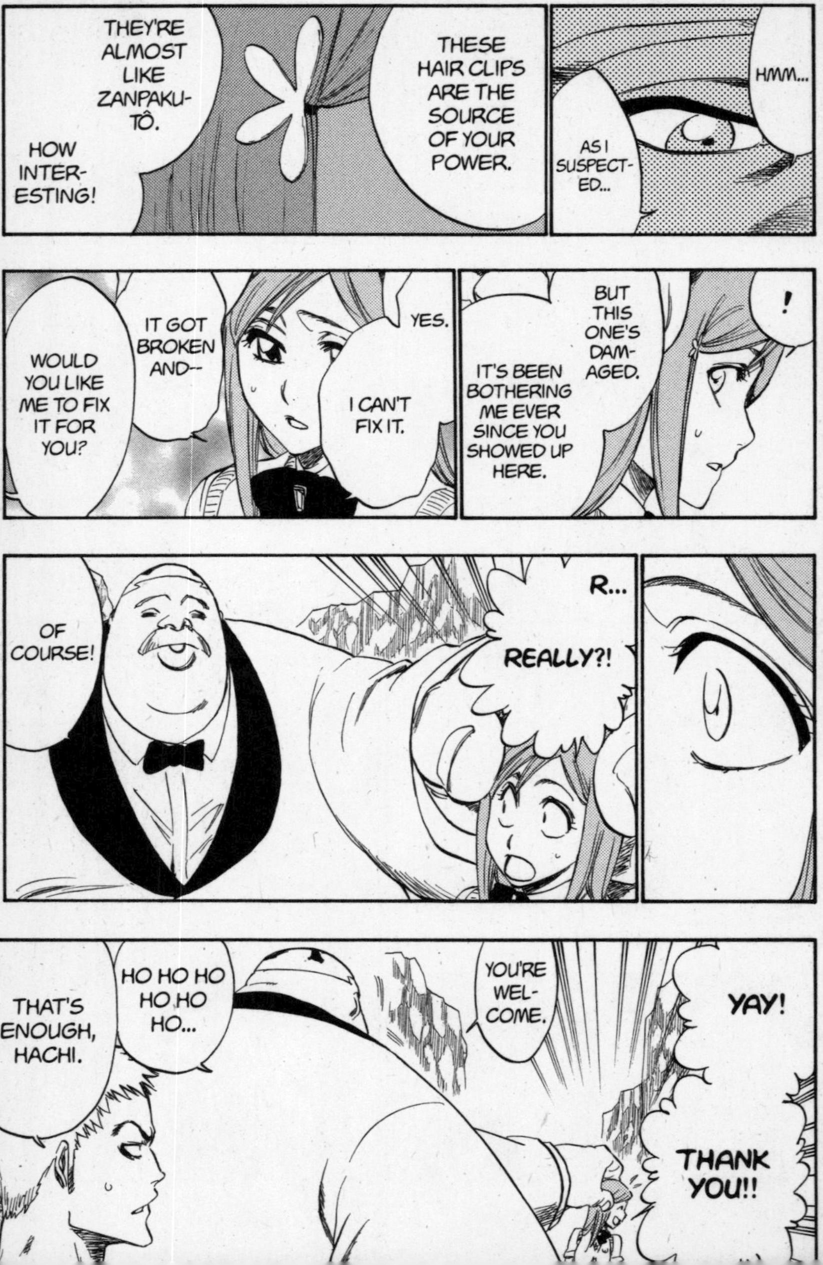

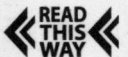

DOOM
I'M HACHIGEN ISHÔDA...
CALL ME HACHI.
IT'S NICE TO MEET YOU.
IT'S...
...NICE TO MEET YOU TOO.
HMM...
STARE
SWAY
HMM...
HMM...
...
UM...
TUMP
WHAT WAS IT YOU WANTED TO...
OWWWWWW!!
MY HEAD! MY HEAD!! YOU'RE GONNA TWIST IT OFF!!

READ THIS WAY

WHAT?

WHO'S HACHI?

HACHI SAYS HE NEEDS YOU!

YOU'RE COMING WITH ME!

WOOOOO

...

WHO WAS THAT?!

WHO...

WAH! WA...

SHOOO M

WA...

THW

UMP

OUCH!!

THUD
WHAT ?!
HI-
HIYORI?!
WHAP

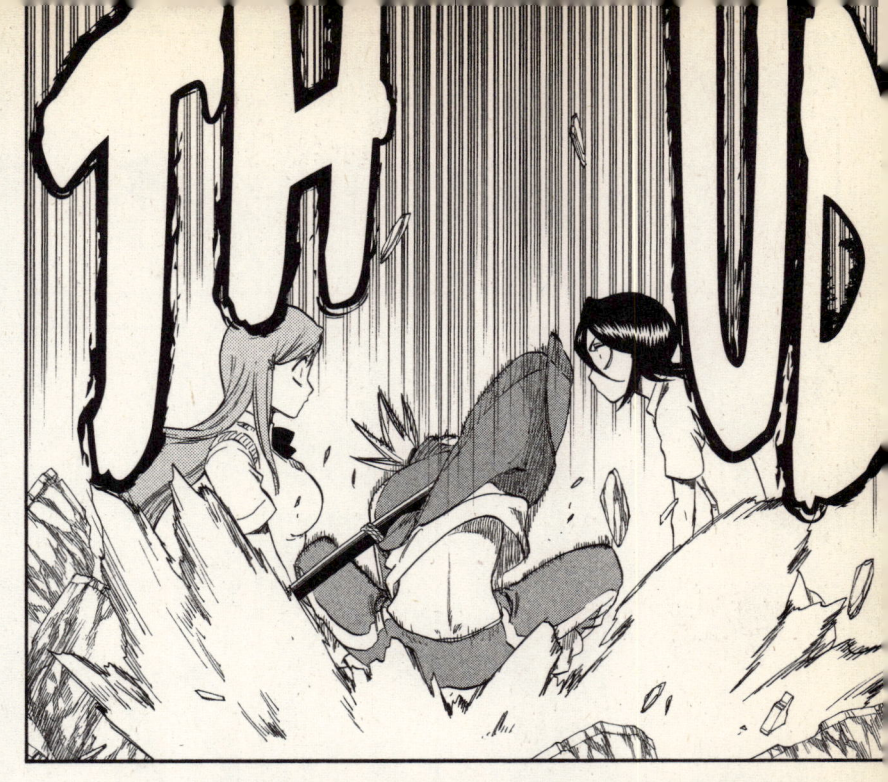

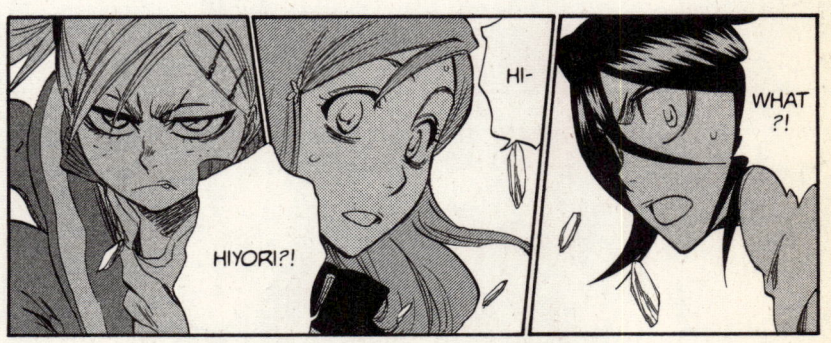

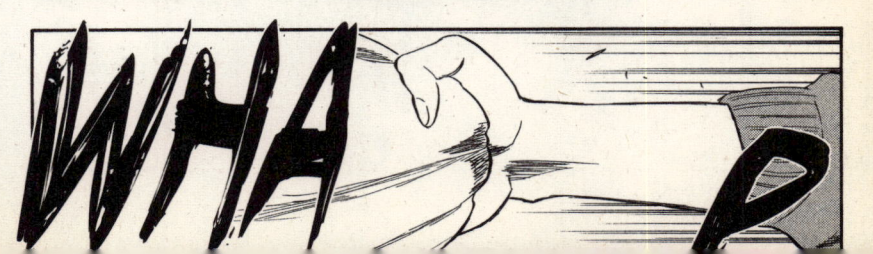

NOT ONE OF YOU...
...WAS A HINDRANCE IN THE BATTLE AT THE SOUL SOCIETY.
NOT ICHIGO...
OR CHAD...
OR URYÛ...
AND, ORIHIME...
...NEITHER WERE YOU.
IF ANY ONE OF YOU HADN'T BEEN THERE...
...I'D BE DEAD NOW.
THERE HAS TO BE SOME-THING YOU CAN DO...
...TO MAKE YOURSELF FIT FOR THIS BATTLE.
LET'S FIND IT TOGETHER.
OKAY?
RUKIA...

...I'D RATHER BE SAD.

LISTEN... ...ORI-HIME.

IT'S NOT THE WEAK OF BODY...

...THAT CAUSE PROBLEMS ON THE BATTLEFIELD.

IT'S THE WEAK OF SPIRIT.

YOU'VE DONE YOUR SHARE OF FIGHTING UP TO NOW!!
YOU EVEN WENT TO THE SOUL SOCIETY AND FOUGHT !!
DOESN'T IT MAKE YOU MAD...
...TO BE DISMISSED LIKE THAT ?!
I...
I'M NOT...
STOP LYING!!
I...
I'M NOT LYING!
AND I'M NOT MAD!
I'M JUST...
I'M JUST SAD.
I WANT TO FIGHT WITH THE REST OF YOU!
BUT...
...MORE IMPORTANT-LY...
...I DON'T WANT TO BE A BURDEN TO ANYONE.
IF I'M GOING TO...
...HINDER ICHIGO OR ANYONE ELSE...

WHAT?!

IT'S OKAY.

I FEEL BETTER AFTER TALKING WITH YOU.

NO.

URAHARA SAID THAT?! THAT JERK!

YOU POOR THING...

IT'S NOT OKAY!!

IT'S FOR THE BEST.

HE'S RIGHT. I'M NOT STRONG ENOUGH.

WHAP

228. Don't Look Back

Bleach 228.
Don't Look Back

ORIHIME?
WHAT'S WRONG?
YOU LOOK SO...
RU...
RUKIA...
SNIFF
HUH ?!
H-HEY! WHAT IS IT, ORIHIME ?!
ORIHIME!!

228. Don't Look Back

TMP TMP TMP TMP TMP TMP TMP TMP
TMP TMP TMP TMP TMP
SH HUK
!

HMM... ISN'T IT KIND OF FLASHY?
BUT THEN THIS IS A SPECIAL TRIP.
BUT MY BELLY-BUTTON WILL SHOW. HOW EMBARRASSING.
A NAME-TAG?!
I'M BUSY! I DON'T HAVE TIME TO SEW ONE ON FOR YOU!
GEEZ... IF YOU'D TOLD ME EARLIER I WOULD'VE PUT SOMETHING LIKE "FAT SOW" ON IT!

THAT'S AN INTERESTING ABILITY YOU HAVE...

...GIRL.

80

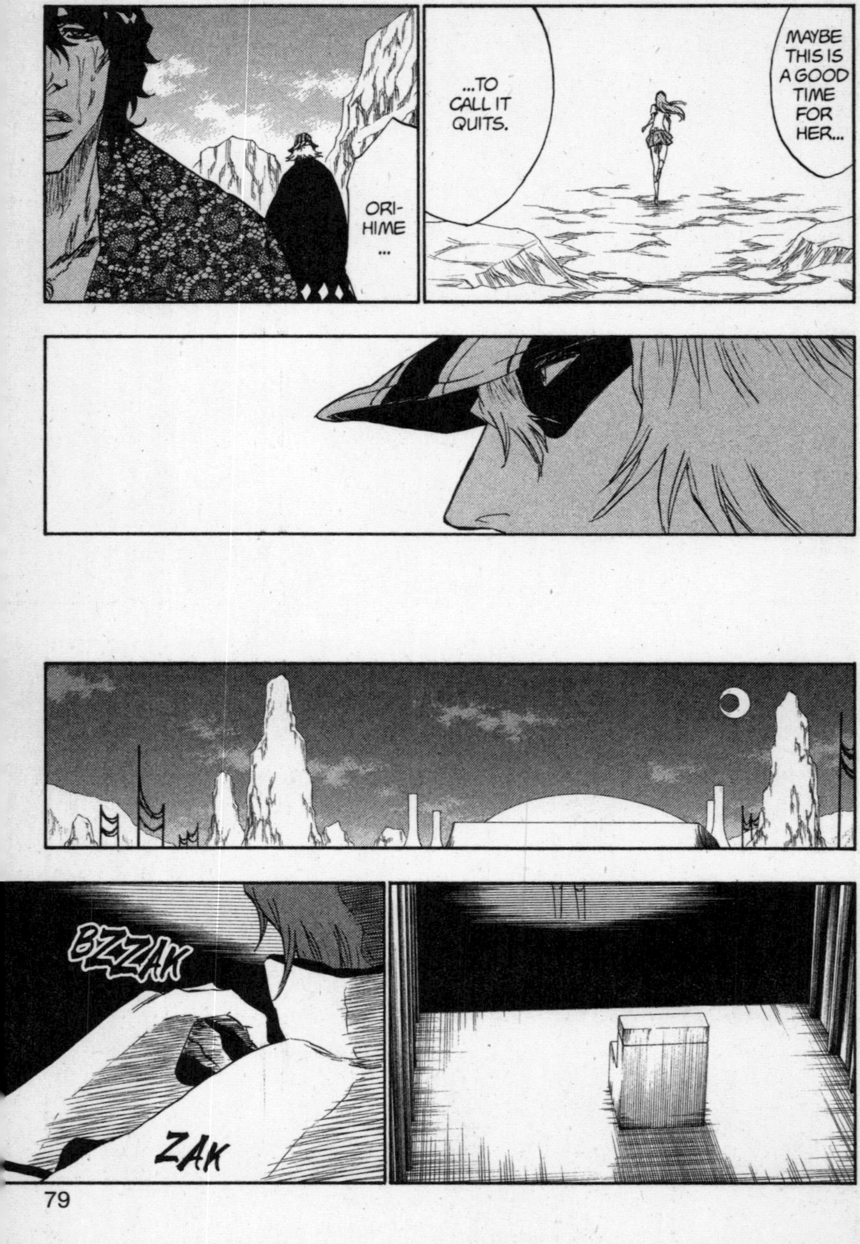

GOOD-BYE!
DASH
ORI-HIME!!
WHAP
RENJI?
DON'T.
URAHARA'S RIGHT.
FOURTH COMPANY MAY SPECIALIZE IN HEALING, BUT THEY'VE ALSO HAD COMBAT TRAINING.
ORIHIME MAY HAVE SOME ABILITIES, BUT SHE'S STILL JUST A HUMAN.
AND TAKING INTO ACCOUNT HER PERSON-ALITY...
SHE JUST WASN'T MEANT TO BE A WARRIOR.

READ THIS WAY

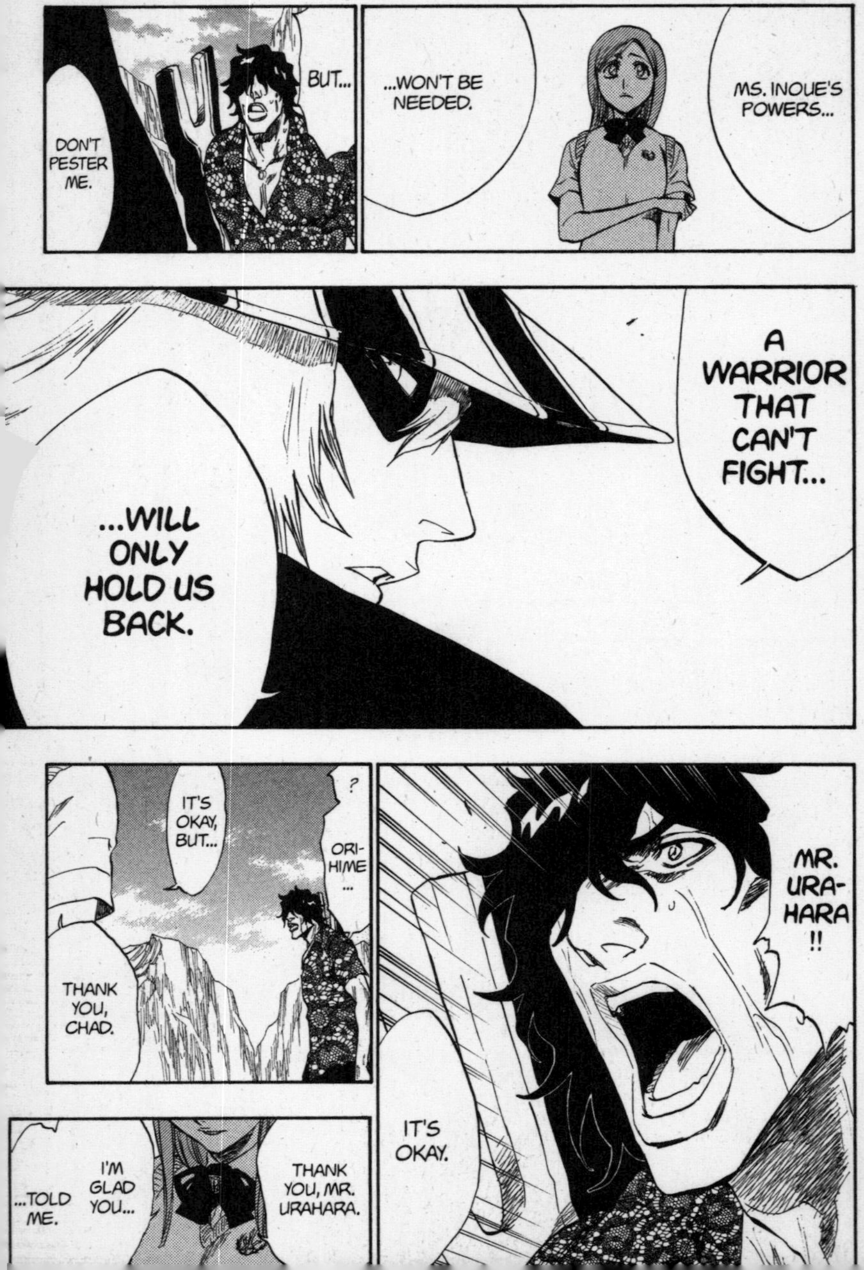

WHOA...
TMP
HOLD ON, MR. URAHARA!
SHE'S A FRIEND OF OURS.
SHE FOUGHT HARD IN THE SOUL SOCIETY.
NOW SHE WANTS TO GET STRONGER.
WE CAN'T JUST LEAVE HER BEHIND!
CHAD...
THAT'S AN EMOTIONAL ARGUMENT.
DO YOU WANT HER TO GET KILLED?
NO!
BUT SHE'S GOT AN ABILITY MORE VALUABLE THAN FIGHTING...
SHE CAN PROTECT AND HEAL PEOPLE!
THE SANTEN-KESSHUN'S DEFENSIVE CAPABILITIES ARE LIMITED.
IT WON'T BE USEFUL IN THIS UPCOMING BATTLE.
FOURTH COMPANY CAN TAKE CARE OF OUR CASUALTIES.
AND WE'LL HAVE PEOPLE LIKE CAPTAIN UNOHANA AND ASSISTANT CAPTAIN KOTETSU WITH US ON THE FRONT LINES THIS TIME.

WHAT?

TSU-BAKI...

...WAS DESTROYED IN THE BATTLE WITH THE ARRANCARS THE OTHER DAY.

HAS HE BEEN REPAIRED?

IT'S OUT OF THE QUESTION.

I CAN'T ALLOW YOU TO PARTICIPATE IN THE BATTLE WITHOUT HIM.

TSUBAKI IS YOUR ONLY OFFENSIVE WEAPON.

I DON'T EVEN KNOW HOW TO FIX HIM.

HE WAS BROKEN SO BADLY I COULDN'T FIX HIM.

NO.

YOU WON'T BE...

...FIGHTING WITH US THIS TIME.

IT CAUGHT US ALL BY SURPRISE, I'M AFRAID.

WE AND THE SOUL SOCIETY HAVE TO PREPARE TO FIGHT A BATTLE THIS WINTER...

IN ANY CASE...

I'M SURE THE STORY'S REACHED IKKAKU BY NOW AS WELL.

YOU'VE HEARD, HAVEN'T YOU? ABOUT THE ÔKEN?

...WE'LL ALL NEED TO BE STRONGER THAN EVER BEFORE.

AND...

A GREAT DEAL OF BLOOD WILL BE SHED, MORE THAN EVER BEFORE.

AN ALL-OUT WAR.

RIGHT.

I...

...WANT TO GET STRONGER TOO!

BUT THERE'S SOMETHING I HAVE TO TELL YOU. ORIHIME...

OF COURSE YOU DO.

"You're pushing yourself too hard, tough guy."

"...keep going."

"I can..."

"Mr. Urahara..."

"Rangiku..."

"...of Tenth Company stopped by earlier."

"What is it... ...you wanted to talk to me about?"

TUMP

TESSAI! URURU! CHAD!

URAHARA!! HE'S EXHAUSTED!

I'M CALLING IT A DAY!

WHUP

WA... WAIT.

KLAK

PLEASE REVIVE CHAD.

WHAM
PLEASE, PLEASE!
HAVE A SEAT!
KRASH
OOF
WELL, I'VE BEEN WATCHING TWO SWEATY GUYS WAIL ON EACH OTHER FOR DAYS NOW...
...SO IT'S NICE HAVING A YOUNG WOMAN STOP BY THE OFFICE.
WHAM
AGH!!
UM...
MR. URA-HARA...
CHAD?
RENJI?
KLAK KLAK KLAK
KLAK

WELL...

HARA SHŌTEN

IT'S BEEN A LONG TIME. ♪

HELLO THERE, MS. INOUE!

UH-HUH...

KARAKURA 1ST HIGH SCHOOL
24TH STUDENT COUNCIL PRESIDENT
Karakura 1st High
Student Council

BLEACH 227. The Swordless Soldier

SLAM

HONEY, I'M HOME!

HAVE YOU BEEN A GOOD BOY?!

OH...

HEY... TAKE IT EASY ON THE BOY. HE ONLY WANTED TO JUMP YOU.

KLUNK

SORRY. REFLEX.

HEY, WAIT A MINUTE!!

IS EVERYONE AROUND HERE LIKE THEM?

LOOK, IT'S GOING TO GET MESSY, SO DO WHAT YOU CAME HERE TO DO AND GO.

SHUT UP

WHAT DO YOU WANT?

I COULDN'T MISTAKE MY OWN HOUSE! WHO THE HECK ARE YOU PEOPLE?!

SORRY.

WRONG DOOR.

THWA
WHAM
!
SHRSHHH
HEH HEH... I'VE BEEN UNDER-ESTIMATED.
I, KEIGO ASANO...
...WILL NEVER FALL FOR THE SAME TECHNI--
CHUNK
GACK!!

READ THIS WAY
REALLY?
I COMPLAIN LIKE CRAZY. ABOUT THE FOOD, THE CLOTHES...
WHO'S THE POOR SUCKER SHE'S STAYING WITH?
YOU KNOW. THAT GIRL.
ORIHIME.
SHE MAY BE A MORTAL, BUT EVEN I'M STARTING TO FEEL SORRY FOR HER.
CHAK
HELLO...
I'M HOME!
MR. IKKAKU, MR. YUMI-CHIKA...
HOW IS EVERY-
-THING?
KREEK
DOOM
YAHOO!!
I MUST BE DREAMING! IT'S THE SECOND COMING OF THE GODDESS OF BREASTS!!
EVEN CLOTHES CAN'T HIDE THEM! OH, THE NAUGHTI-NESS!!

HA HA HA HA HA HA HA!!
ZANG
M-M-MATSUMOTO?! HOW'D YOU GET IN HERE?!
THE FRONT DOOR.
IT WAS OPEN.
DON'T YOU HAVE ANY SECURITY IN THIS PLACE?
BUT MORE IMPORTANTLY...
...WHAT HAS THIS WORLD DONE TO YOUR FASHION SENSE?
I GOT THIS FROM THE LANDLADY!
YOU JUST WEAR WHATEVER THE LANDLADY GIVES YOU?!
OF COURSE!!
WE'VE GOT FREE ROOM AND BOARD HERE! YOU THINK I'M GONNA COMPLAIN ABOUT THE CLOTHES SHE GIVES ME?!

227. The Swordless Soldier

OH, WOW!!
YOU LOOK SO CUTE!!
HA HA HA HA HA HA HA!!
WHAT LOUSY TASTE!
KRAK
NOW SHUT UP.
AND STOP SCREAM-ING.

THE BEACH ?!
YAY!! WATERMELON!!
SERIOUSLY ?!
I'D BETTER GO BUY A NEW SWIM-SUIT. ♡

TMP
WHY?
WHY DIDN'T YOU USE HAIZEN?
IF YOU'D USED HAIZEN INSTEAD OF GRITZ...
...YOU MAY NOT HAVE DEFEATED ME, BUT YOU MIGHT'VE AT LEAST INFLICTED A WOUND.
YOU MADE A STUPID CHOICE.
YOU MAKE ME SICK.
BUT...
I'LL LET YOU LIVE THIS TIME.

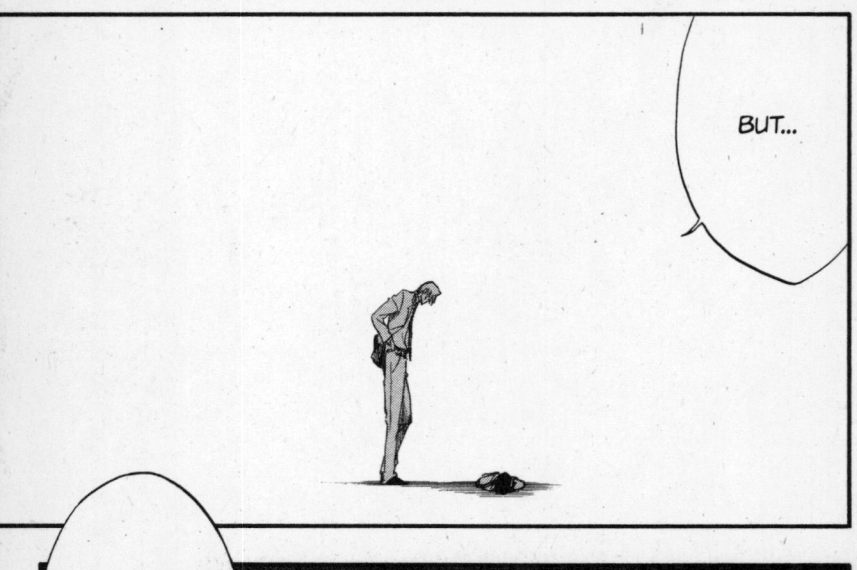

THAT...

...IS THE ONLY WAY TO REGAIN THE SPIRITUAL POWERS LOST WHILE IN...

...QUINCY LETZ STILE. (FINAL FORM)

THUD

KLAK

KLINK

YOU HAVE TO PUSH YOUR MIND AND BODY TO THEIR LIMITS...

KLAK

KLAK

...BE STRUCK BY A SPIRIT ARROW 19 MM TO THE RIGHT OF THE HEART'S SINOATRIAL NODE.

...AND WHILE IN THAT CONDITION...

DOOM

UGH...

HE GOT ME.

WHAT?!

DOOM

I'M SORRY.

IT'S OVER.

YES!!

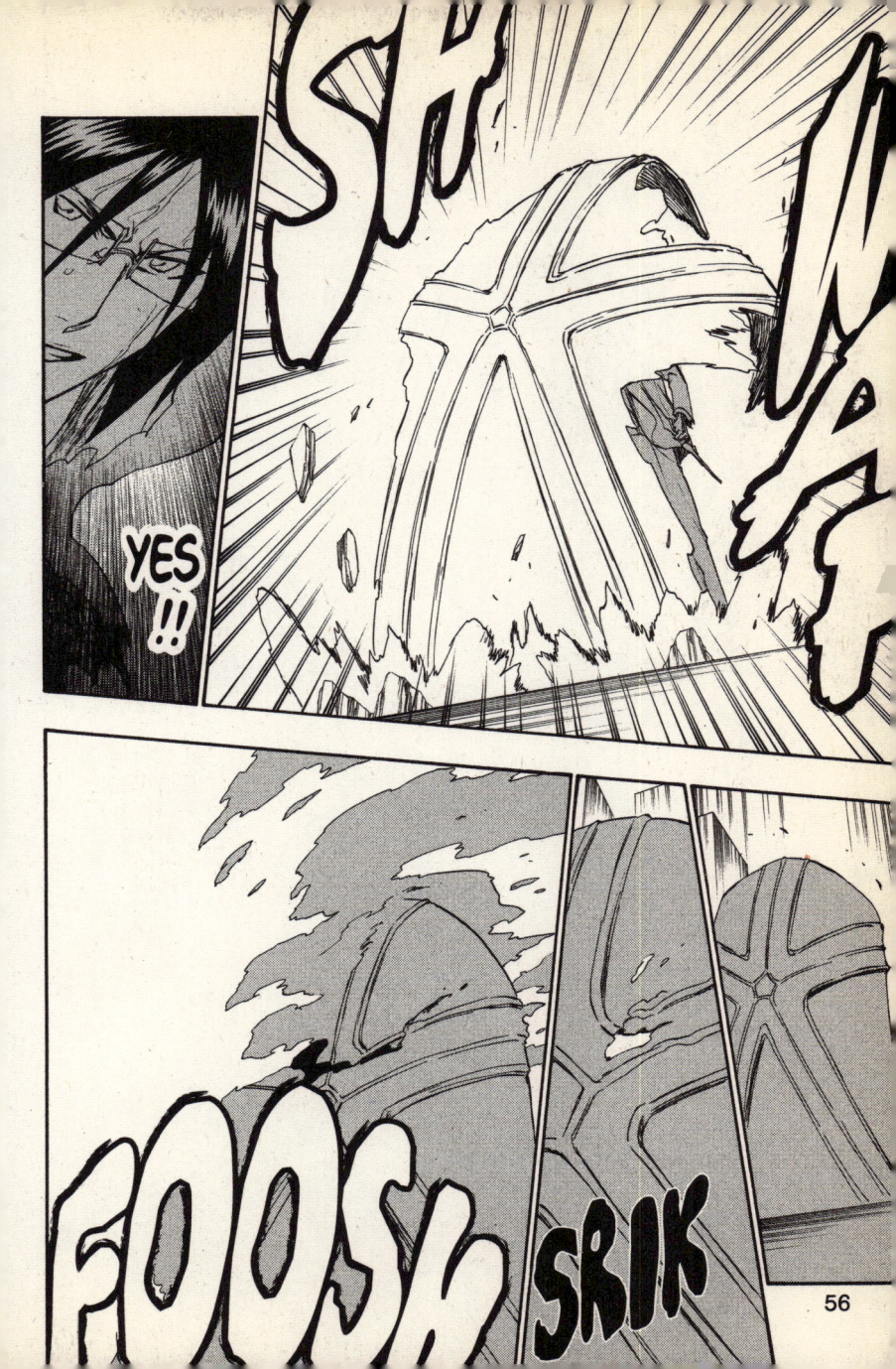

FOOSH

SRIK

I'VE REACHED MY LIMIT.
I HAVE TO IMMOBILIZE HIM AND END THIS EXERCISE!
AND NOW'S...
...MY CHANCE!
TUMP
!
MY LAST GINTÔ!
THE SILVER WHIP STRIKES THE FIVE-FINGERED STONE BED!
GRITZ!
(FIVE-PRONGED RESTRAINT)
TUNK

FOOM FOOM FOOM FOOM

MY LIMIT?

I CAN BARELY MOVE MY ARMS AND LEGS.

RRMMM

TMP TMP

HE TOLD ME THAT IF I KEPT DODGING HIS ARROWS I'D REGAIN MY POWERS, BUT THERE'S NO SIGN THAT IT'S WORKING.

WAS HE LYING TO ME?

BUT IF WE KEEP GOING LIKE THIS, HE'LL KILL ME.

BUT HIS SPIRITUAL PRESSURE IS WEAKENING TOO.

RRMMMMMMM

TMP

HAVE YOU REACHED YOUR LIMIT?!

YOU'RE SLOWING DOWN!

YOU CALL THAT DODGING?!

WHAT'S THE MATTER?

SO YOU HAD SOME GINTÔ STASHED AWAY.

ARE YOU CALLING ME...

...A COWARD?

HOW VERY CAUTIOUS OF YOU.

EXACTLY.

!
SWIP
SH...
SHOOT!
WHUP
OOOOOOOOOOOO
TILT THE GOBLET TO THE WEST!
WOLKE!! (EMERALD CHALICE)
THOOM

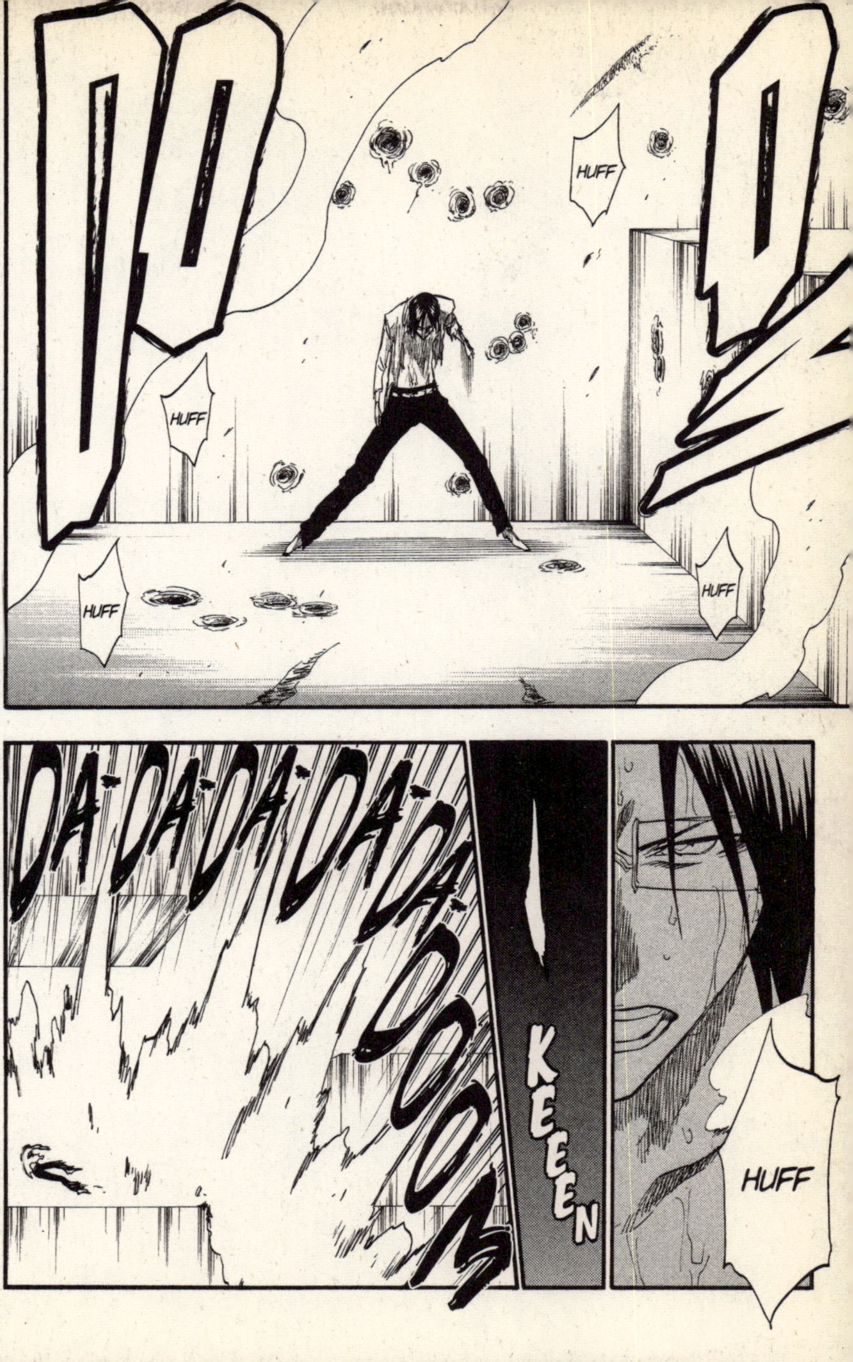
DO
O
HUFF
HUFF
HUFF
HUFF
DA DA DA DA DA DA DOOOOM
KEEEN
HUFF

HE WANTS ME TO BRING YOU...

...TO HIS UNDER-GROUND TRAINING ROOM RIGHT AWAY.

BLEACH

226. Right of My Heart

GENERAL
HOSPITAL

HUFF...
HUFF...
TMP
HUFF...

WOO

...ORI-HIME.

THERE YOU ARE...

MS. YORUICHI!

KISUKE SENT ME...

...TO FIND YOU.

READ THIS WAY

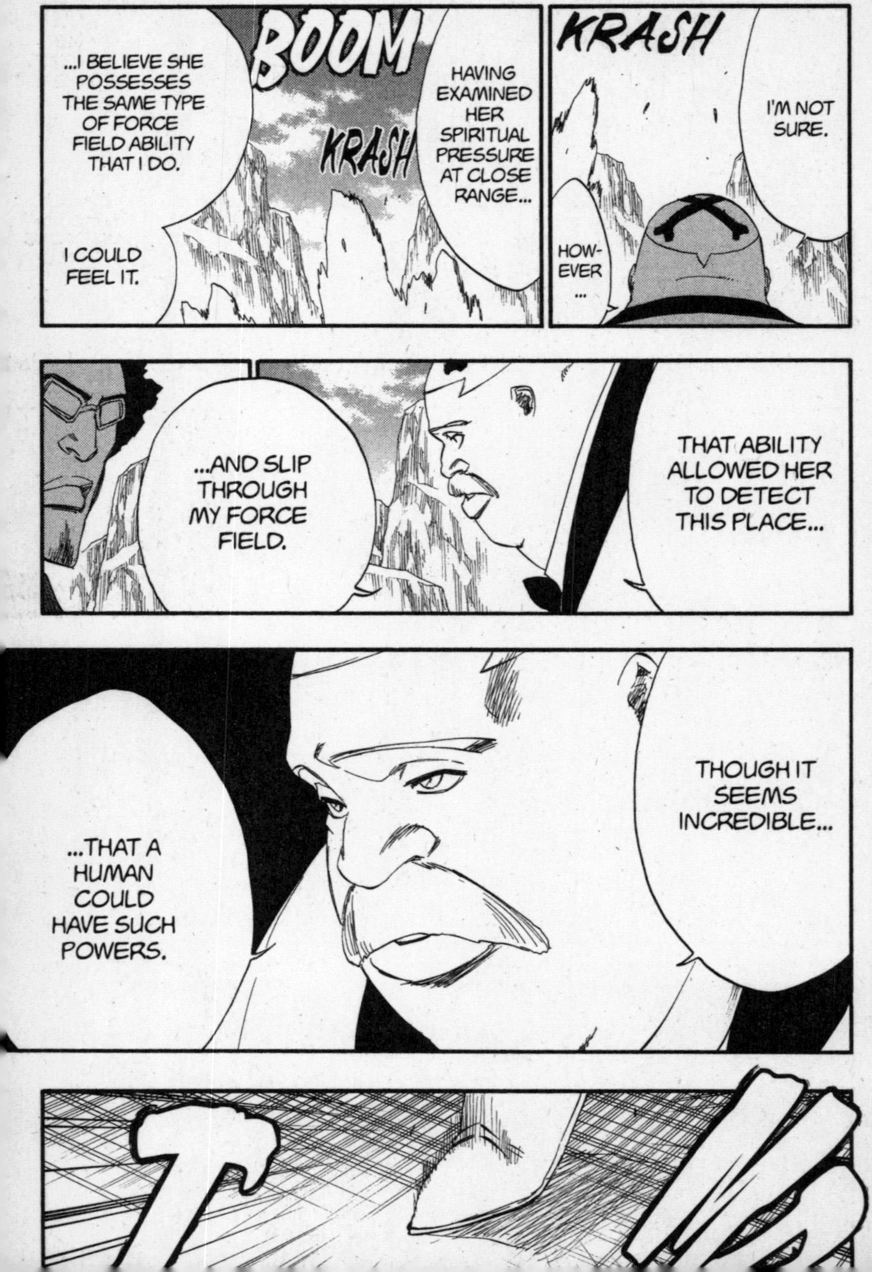

| KRA-DOOM WHOA!! DON'T TAKE YOUR EYES OFF ME!! | THAT'S BECAUSE I DIDN'T, DIPSTICK. | HE SAYS THAT ABOUT EVERY PRETTY GIRL?! I DON'T REMEMBER HIM SAYING THAT ABOUT ME!! |

YES?

HACHI...

OF COURSE.

YOUR FORCE FIELDS ARE FLAWLESS. THERE'S NO DOUBT ABOUT THAT.

...AND GET INSIDE?

THEN HOW DID ORIHIME DETECT THIS PLACE...

HEY...
WHO WAS THAT GIRL?!
SHE JUST SPOKE TO ICHIGO AND RAN AWAY.
IT LOOKED LIKE THEY WERE FRIENDS.
THAT WAS...
...ORIHIME.
HUH?!
WHAT?! YOU KNOW HER?!
ORIHIME WAS...
...MY FIRST LOVE.
WHAT AN OBVIOUS LIE.
YOU SAY THAT ABOUT EVERY PRETTY GIRL...
INCLUD-ING ME.
IS SHE SAYING SHE'S PRETTY?

226: Right of My Heart

UM...
THAT SOUNDS LIKE FUN, BUT I CAN'T GO.
WHY NOT?
I DON'T HAVE A BATHING SUIT.
IT'S A SIZE ISSUE.
OH, NO!
THEN LET'S GO BUY YOU ONE RIGHT NOW...
...IN THE WORLD OF THE LIVING!
WHAT?
WA...
WAIT, CAPTAIN UNO-HANA!
CALL ME CHAIR-WOMAN HERE.
HERE?! WE'RE IN THE BAR-RACKS!

...GET STRONGER TOO!

I HAVE TO...

TMP

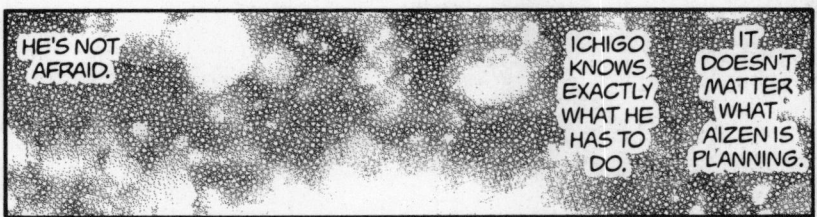

...BECAUSE HE'S SO BUSY TRAINING AND GETTING STRONGER.

HE CAN'T REALLY PROCESS WHAT I TOLD HIM...

THAT'S MS. HIYORI, BALDY!!

ALL RIGHT! LET'S GET BACK TO TRAINING, HIYORI!

I SEE.

HE'S NOT AFRAID.

ICHIGO KNOWS EXACTLY WHAT HE HAS TO DO.

IT DOESN'T MATTER WHAT AIZEN IS PLANNING.

...AND NOT IN A SCARY WAY LIKE BEFORE...

...GETTING REALLY STRONG...

ICHIGO'S...

AND NOW...

IT'S A STRANGE WAY.

BUT IT'S NOT A NICE WAY, EITHER.

DON'T WORRY.
I'M GONNA STOP AIZEN.
I'M GETTING STRONGER.
I CAN...
...FEEL IT.
THANKS FOR THE HEADS-UP...
...ORIHIME.

I SEE.

...

WHAT?

...

OH... I MEAN...

YOU DON'T SEEM VERY SURPRISED BY WHAT I TOLD YOU.

TMP

BUT IT'S OKAY.

...I JUST FOUND OUT THAT KARAKURA'S GOING TO BE WIPED OUT BECAUSE OF THIS ŌKEN THING, AND... I'M JUST HAVING A HARD TIME WRAPPING MY HEAD AROUND IT.

IT'S JUST THAT...

SURE I AM.

E-EXCUSE ME...
WHERE'S THE BATHROOM?
JUST KIDDING.
HUH?!
GRR
THAT WAS A JOKE.
SHE SAID SHE WAS KIDDING.
WHAT DO YOU THINK, KENSEI?
IF IT WERE ME, I WOULDN'T BE JOKING AROUND IN A SITUATION LIKE THIS.
!
THUD
WHAT ARE YOU DOING, ICHIGO?!
KRUNCH
UGH!
CRAP...
ICHIGO!!
ORIHIME?!

SHWO

STARE

UM... UH...

IT'S A... ...HUMAN?!

!!...
A SOUL REAPER?
NO.
THE HACHIGYÔ SÔGAI (TWIN CLIFFS) I SET IS AN ORIGINAL TECHNIQUE I DEVELOPED AFTER I BECAME A VISORED.
IT CAN'T BE BROKEN BY A SOUL REAPER'S KIDÔ.
THEN WHO IS IT?! ANOTHER VISORED?!
I DON'T KNOW.
NOT EVEN A VISORED SHOULD BE ABLE TO DO THAT.
THE STRANGE THING IS THAT THEY DIDN'T BREAK THROUGH THE FORCE FIELD. THEY **SLIPPED** THROUGH.
THEN...
...WHO OR **WHAT** IS IT?
OOOO
WOOO
IT'S COMING.
...
TMP

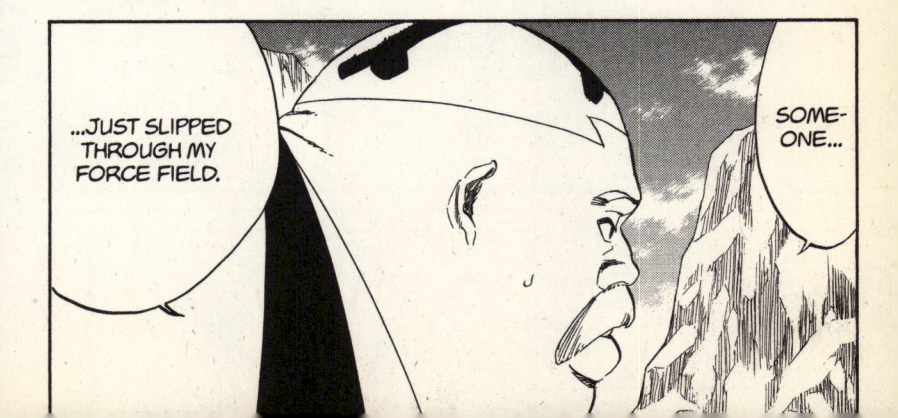

BO **NG**

WH U

WHAT'S UP, HACHI?

SOME-ONE...

...JUST SLIPPED THROUGH MY FORCE FIELD.

...DOING THIS ANYWAY?

SO, HEY...

WHY'S BERRY BOY...

WHOA, THAT'S SHORT!

FOUR SECONDS.

IT'S TRUE.

WHAT? LIAR.

NO, I DIDN'T.

YOU DID IT TOO.

HE'S TRAINING TO INCREASE THE LENGTH OF TIME THAT HE CAN REMAIN HOLLOW-FIED.

SHE'S THE ONLY ONE WHO HASN'T DONE THIS PART OF THE TRAINING.

MASHIRO WAS ABLE TO HOLLOWFY FOR OVER 15 HOURS FROM THE VERY START.

NOW, NOW...

WHY, YOU!!

KENSEI, YOU GROUCH! YOU'RE A JERK!

SEE?!

BLEH

HMPH

REALLY? GUESS I FORGOT.

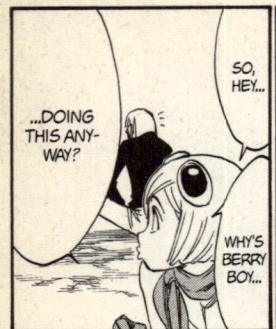

KROOM KROOM

KRASH

WELL, IT'S NOT EASY.

HIS RETENTION TIME ISN'T INCREASING VERY QUICKLY.

WHACK
OW!!
HOW MANY TIMES DO I HAVE TO TELL YOU--YOU'RE SLOWER IMMEDIATELY AFTER YOU HOLLOWFY!!
IF THAT FIRST BLOW OF MINE HAD LANDED, YOU'D BE DEAD!!
TOMP TOMP TOMP TOMP
STOMP

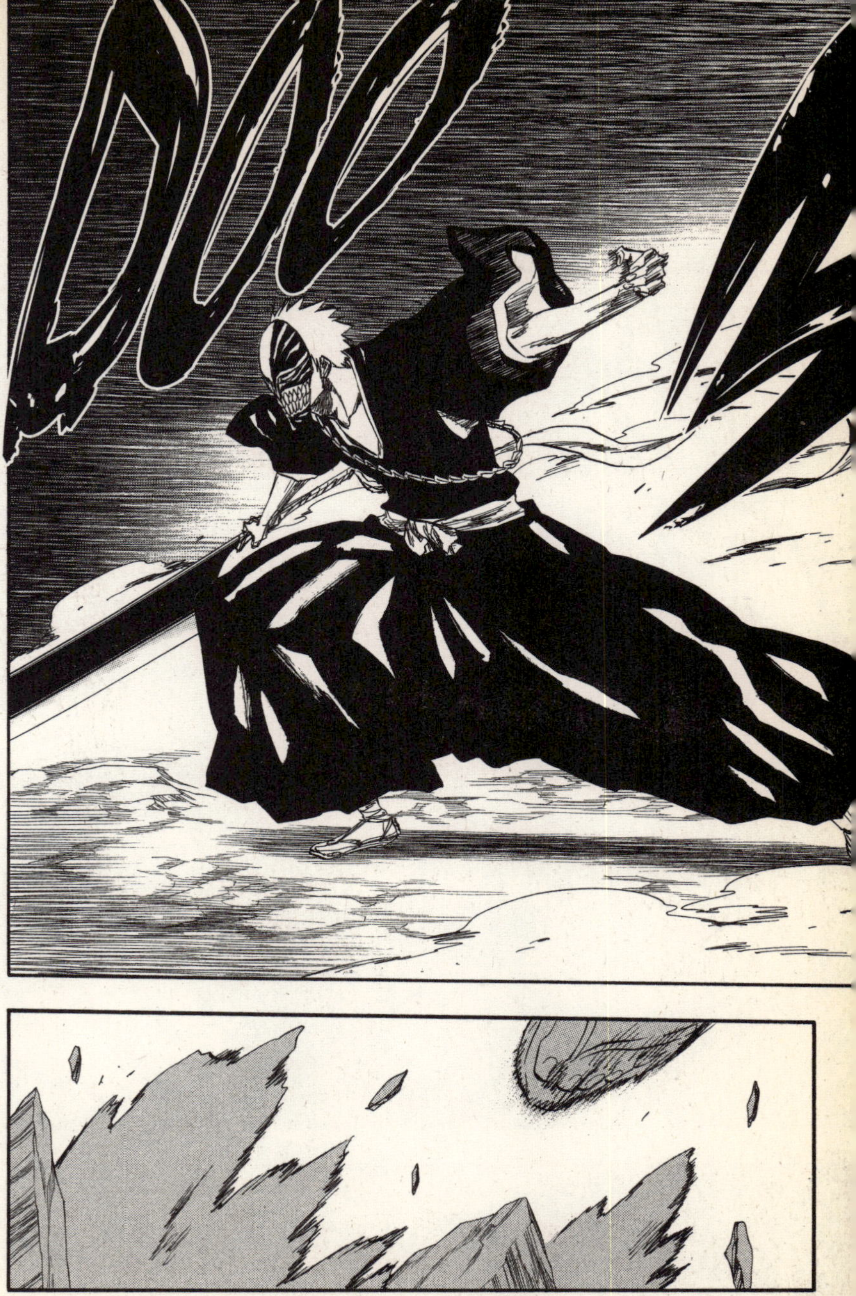

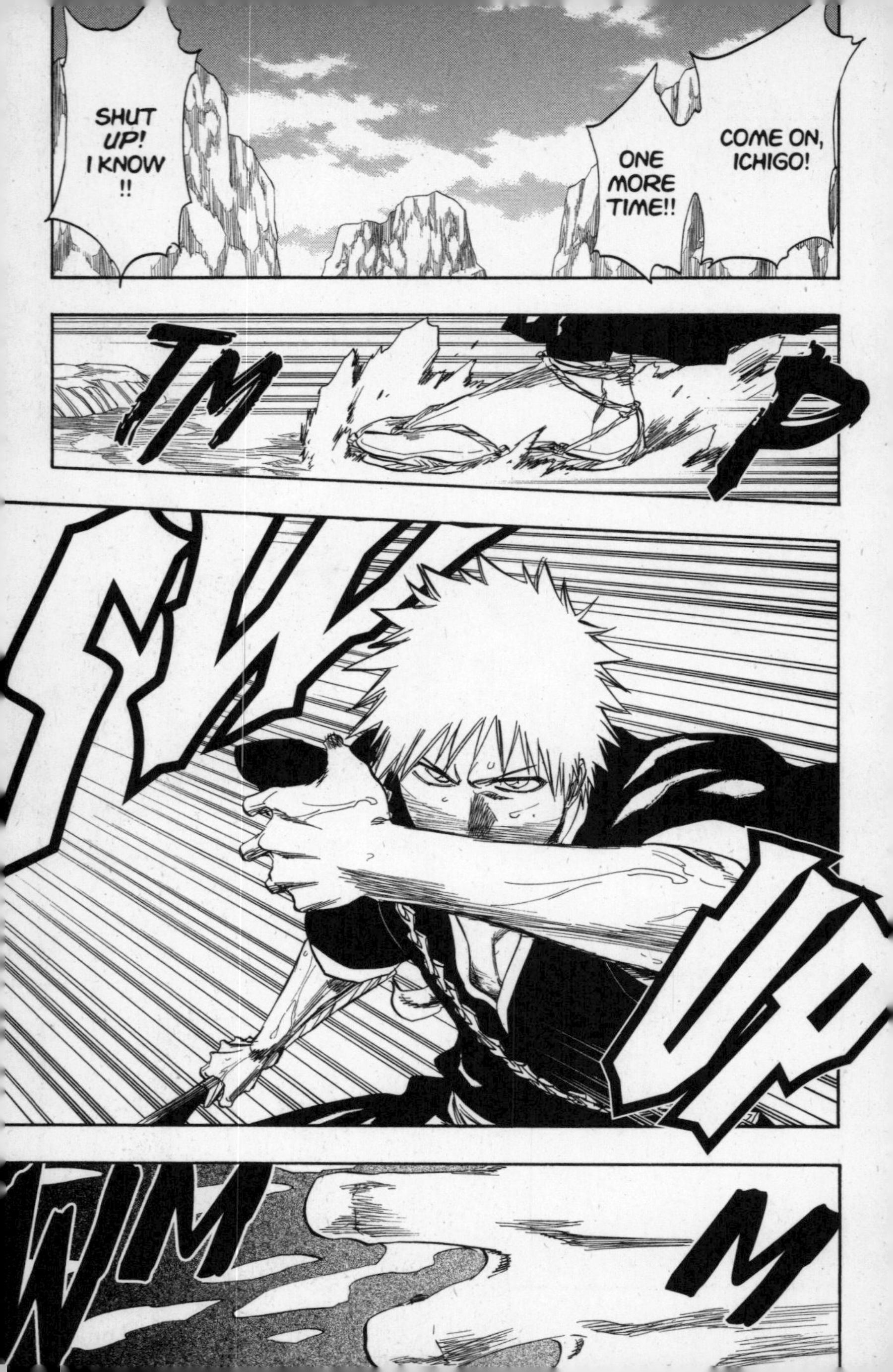

COME ON, ICHIGO!
ONE MORE TIME!!
SHUT UP! I KNOW !!
TMP
SWUP
WMM

BLEACH 225. Slip into My Barrier

井上織姫

ORIHIME INOUE

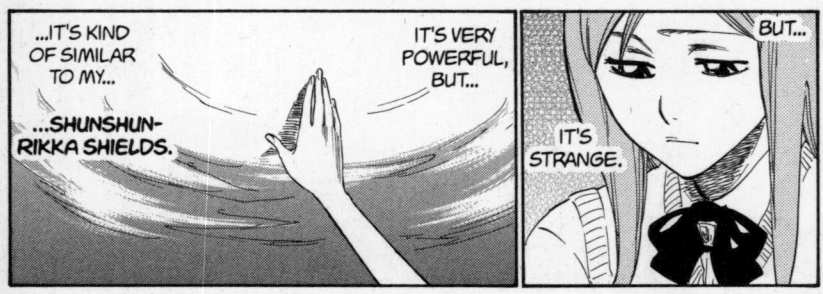

TING

...IT'S KIND OF SIMILAR TO MY...

...SHUNSHUN- RIKKA SHIELDS.

IT'S VERY POWERFUL, BUT...

BUT...

IT'S STRANGE.

VWM

I CAN PUT MY HAND THROUGH IT.

...

THEY CAN'T GO NEAR IT...
...BECAUSE THERE'S A FORCE FIELD THERE.
IT'S BLOCKING THIS BUILDING OUT OF PEOPLE'S MINDS. THEY DON'T EVEN KNOW IT'S HERE.
THEY CAN'T EVEN THINK OF APPROACHING IT.
AMAZING.

THAT CAT LOOKS LIKE IT'S WALKING NEXT TO AN INVISIBLE WALL.
THOSE BIRDS TOO...
NOTHING WILL GO NEAR IT.
NO.

225. Slip into My Barrier

SOCIETY OF FEMALE SOUL REAPERS CHAIRWOMAN: RETSU UNOHANA
WE COULD ALL USE A LITTLE BREAK, SO...
...LET'S TAKE A TRIP TO THE WORLD OF THE LIVING AND GO TO THE BEACH!
A TRIP ?!
YEAH.

THEY'RE GETTING ALONG SWIMMINGLY.

IDIOT!! THAT'S THE WHOLE POINT OF THIS TRAINING! IF YOU'RE NOT GONNA DO IT RIGHT, THEN DON'T DO IT AT ALL!!

WHAT?!

YEAH.

ARE YOU STUPID OR SOMETHING?! I'D BE IN BIG TROUBLE IF I'D STAYED HOLLOWFIED!!

WOOOOOOOOO

TMP

THAT HAS TO BE IT.

...

AAAAAAAH!!

KRAK

OOF!!

THWAK

I TOLD YOU TO STAY HOLLOWFIED, BALDY!!

YOUR POWERS CLEARLY HAVE THE POTENTIAL TO INCREASE.

MR. SADO...

BUT ONE THING TROUBLES ME...

REPEATED BATTLES AGAINST BANKAI WILL RAISE THEM TO NEW HEIGHTS.

YES, IT'S AS IF YOUR POWERS ARE...

YOUR POWERS AREN'T LIKE THOSE OF SOUL REAPERS OR QUINCIES...

TRAINING SOMEONE IN BANKAI ISN'T AN ODD JOB! TR–

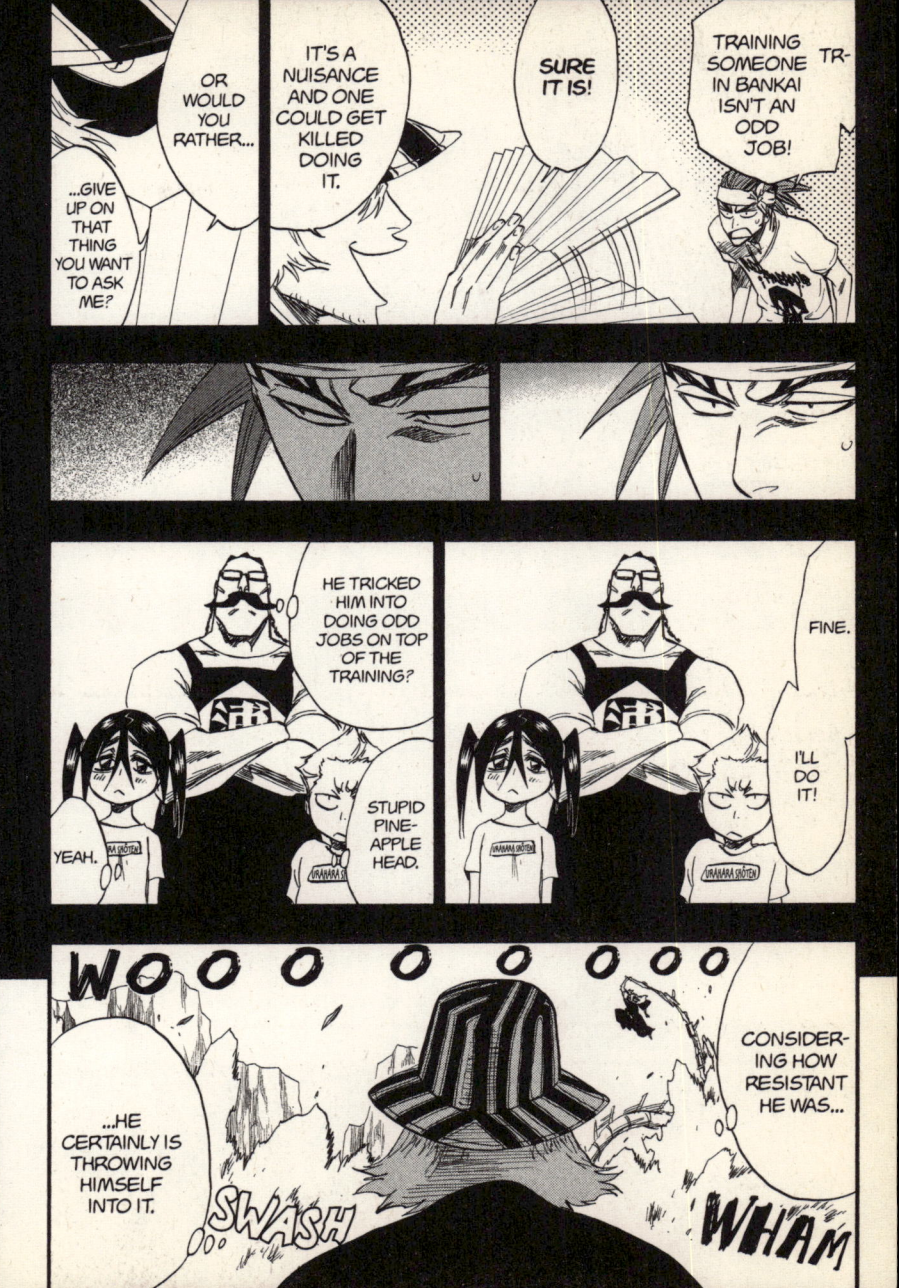

SURE IT IS!

IT'S A NUISANCE AND ONE COULD GET KILLED DOING IT.

OR WOULD YOU RATHER...

...GIVE UP ON THAT THING YOU WANT TO ASK ME?

HE TRICKED HIM INTO DOING ODD JOBS ON TOP OF THE TRAINING?

YEAH.

STUPID PINEAPPLE HEAD.

FINE.

I'LL DO IT!

WOOOOOOOOO

CONSIDERING HOW RESISTANT HE WAS...

...HE CERTAINLY IS THROWING HIMSELF INTO IT.

SWASH

WHAM

OH, YES. I FORGOT. ♪
LET ME GO!!
I'LL MANGLE HIM!!
I'VE NEVER MET ANYONE SO FRUSTRATING BEFORE IN MY LIFE!!
IT HAS TO BE YOU.
MY BANKAI ISN'T SUITED...
...FOR TRAINING OR GIVING PEOPLE STRENGTH.
...
AHA!
I'VE GOT IT!
HOW ABOUT THIS?
THERE'S SOME-THING YOU WANT TO ASK ME, RIGHT?
UP TO NOW I'VE MANAGED TO WORM MY WAY OUT OF IT, BUT...
GEEZ, YOU'RE LAZY.
LET'S MAKE A DEAL!
IF YOU AGREE TO DO ODD JOBS FOR ME FOR THE NEXT THREE MONTHS...
...I'LL ANSWER ANY QUESTIONS YOU ASK!

WHY ME?!
BECAUSE I DON'T THINK HE'LL LEAVE EVEN IF I TELL HIM TO.
THAT'S NOT WHAT I ASKED!
IF HE WANTS TO BE TRAINED, THEN YOU SHOULD TRAIN HIM!
WHOEVER TRAINS MR. SADO NEEDS THE POWER OF BANKAI.
ALL THE MORE REASON FOR YOU TO TRAIN HIM!
FWUP FWUP
YOU CAN DO BANKAI, CAN'T YOU?!
PUH-LEASE!
I'M JUST A LOWLY-BUT-HANDSOME MERCHANT. HOW COULD I POSSIBLY PERFORM BANKAI?
RIDICULOUS
DON'T GIVE ME THAT LOWLY MERCHANT LINE!!
EVERYBODY KNOWS YOU USED TO BE THE CAPTAIN OF TWELFTH COMPANY AND THAT YOU WERE THE ONE WHO MADE THE HÔGYOKU* IN THE FIRST PLACE!

*BREAKDOWN SPHERE. ALLOWS ARRANCARS TO BE INSTANTANEOUSLY CREATED FROM HOLLOWS.

YOU'RE GETTING WEAK!!

WHAT'S WRONG?!

I'M NOT!

NO...

HELP HIM TRAIN?!

AIZEN.

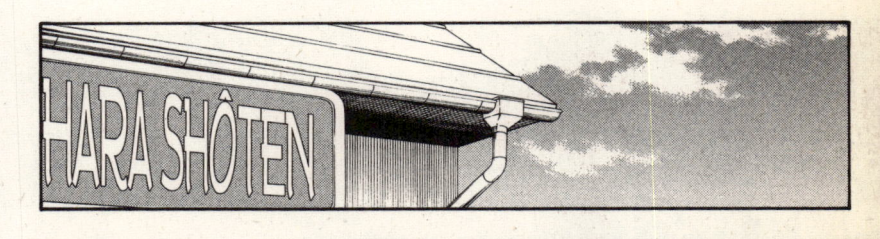

HARA SHÔTEN

GRAAAAH!!

SWUMP
I'M SORRY.
I GRANTED HER REQUEST TO SPEAK WITH YOU...
...BUT IT MAY HAVE BEEN A BIT TOO SOON.
IT'S ALL RIGHT, SIR.
THANK YOU.
CAPTAIN HITSUGAYA ...
GOODBYE, SIR.
ZZT
KSHHHHHHHHHHH
KRK

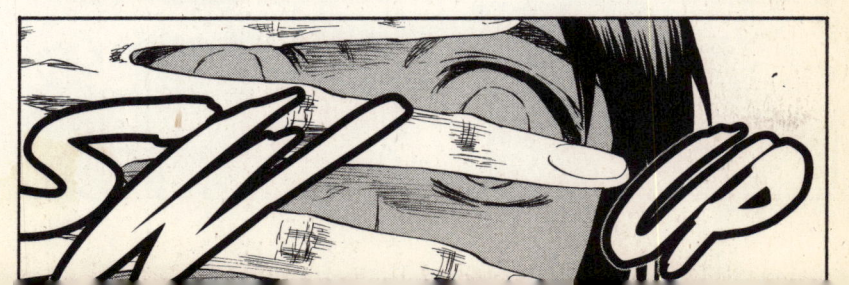

...CAPTAIN AIZEN!

DON'T KILL...

THAT'S IT!

MOMO!

MAYBE CAPTAIN ICHIMARU OR SOMEONE FORCED HIM TO--

BUT HE MUST'VE HAD A REASON!

I KNOW HE DID SOME TERRIBLE THINGS...

WHUP

SHU UP

CAPTAIN ...
CAN I ASK YOU SOMETHING?
WHAT?
...
ARE YOU GOING TO FIGHT...
...CAPTAIN AIZEN?
...
YES.
ARE YOU GOING TO...
...KILL HIM?
PLEASE ...

I'M CAPTAIN HITSUGAYA.

I'M NOT TÔSHIRÔ NOW...

OF COURSE.

YES.

READ THIS WAY

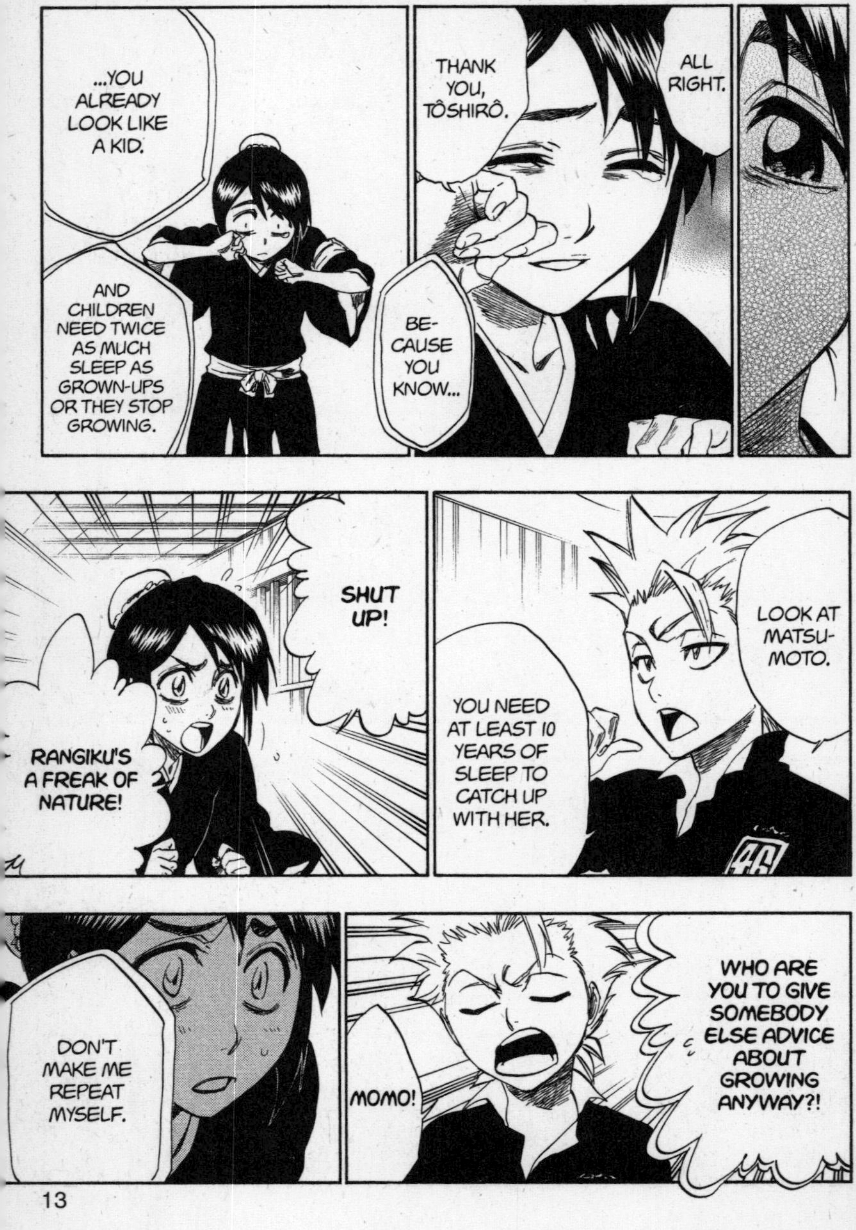

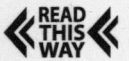

I'M SORRY ...
...I DREW MY SWORD AGAINST YOU.
I DON'T KNOW WHAT I WAS THINKING.
I'M SUCH A--
STOP.
I'VE ALREADY FORGOTTEN ABOUT IT.
IT'S BEHIND US.
IT DOESN'T MATTER.
JUST FORGET ABOUT IT. GO BACK TO SLEEP...
...AND GET RID OF THOSE BAGS UNDER YOUR EYES.

READ THIS WAY

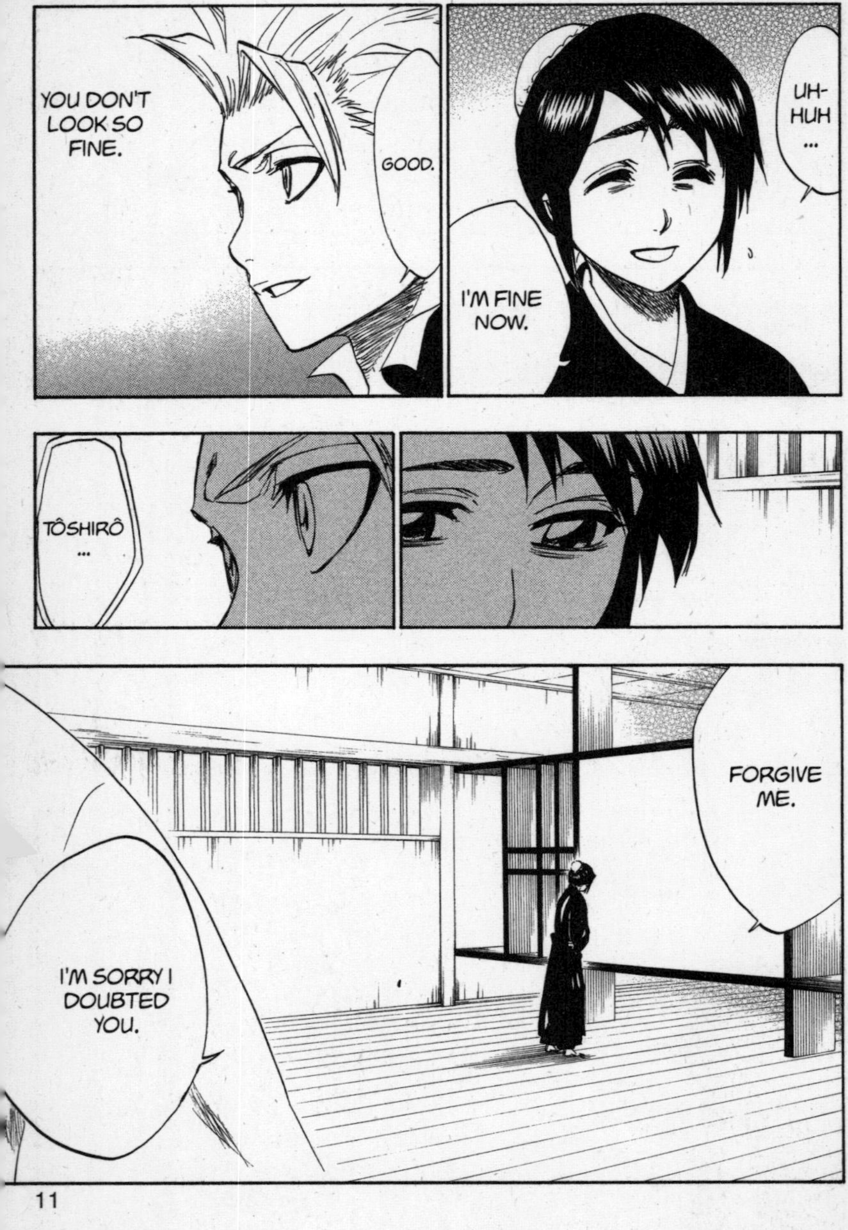

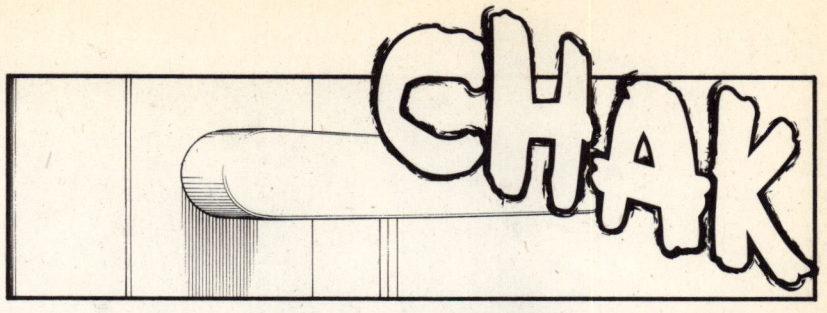

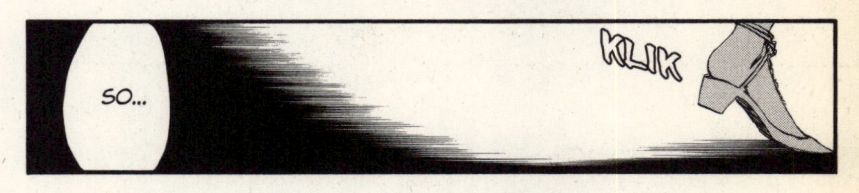

CHAK

SO...

KLIK

YOU'RE AWAKE.

ARE YOU SURE YOU SHOULD BE UP AND AROUND?

MOMO...

224. Imitated Gaiety

BLEACH 224

Imitated Gaiety

TMP

MOMO!

TÔSHIRÔ...

...

224. Imitated Gaiety

TMP

TMP

TMP

TMP

YOU.

...

BLEACH 26

THE MASCARON DRIVE

Contents

224.	Imitated Gaiety	7
225.	Slip into My Barrier	27
226.	Right of My Heart	45
227.	The Swordless Soldier	63
228.	Don't Look Back	83
229.	The Howling Tempest	103
230.	Dead White Invasion	125
231.	The Mascaron Drive	145
232.	The Mascaron Drive 2	164
233.	El Violador	185

BLEACH ALL STORIES

ウルキオラ
Ulquiorra

浦原喜助
Kisuke Urahara

Grimmjow
グリムジョー

STARS AND

Orihime Inoue

井上織姫

Rukia Kuchiki

朽木ルキア

Ichigo Kurosaki

黒崎一護

★ plot

When Ichigo Kurosaki meets Soul Reaper Rukia Kuchiki his life is changed forever, and soon Ichigo becomes a Soul Reaper himself. When Rukia is taken back to the Soul Society for execution, Ichigo saves her and exposes the sinister plot of Sôsuke Aizen in the process. But Aizen escapes to Hueco Mundo, and Ichigo returns to the World of the Living and resumes his work as a Soul Reaper.

Just when Ichigo's life has returned to abnormal, a group of Arrancars—Hollows with the powers of Soul Reapers—makes a foray to his own hometown. The Soul Society, anticipating a large-scale invasion, sends a detachment of Soul Reapers, including Rukia, to the World of the Living. But it soon becomes clear that Aizen's true goal is to create an Ōken, a key that will allow him to assassinate the king of the Soul Society! While Ichigo trains to ready himself for the Arrancars, Orihime races to bring him the news that Karakura is in danger of total destruction!!

The voice that pierces deep into my chest is like a never-ending cheer.

BLEACH 26: THE MASCARON DRIVE

Shonen Jump Manga